# How to

# Prevent

## and

# Defeat Cancer

# Naturally

## E.R. (Ron) Harder
NATURAL HEALTH CONSULTANT

How to Prevent and Defeat Cancer Naturally
Copyright © 2024 by E.R. (Ron) Harder

ISBN
978-1-962868-41-9 (Paperback)
978-1-962868-42-6 (eBook)
978-1-962868-40-2 (Hardcover)

## Disclaimer

This book is not intended as medical advice. All opinions are strictly the opinion of the author and do not constitute medical advice. Consult your health care provider for any questions you may have concerning your health.

Neither the author, publisher, retailer, or anyone else involved with the writing, printing, or distribution of this book shall have any liability, or be responsible to anyone, for any loss, injury, or damage caused by any information contained herein.

# *Table of Contents*

# *About This Book*

This book explains in very simple language WHY we develop cancer, HOW we develop cancer, and what we need to do to defeat any cancer that we may have. It talks about human health in terms that are easy to understand.

It looks at how the process of digestion in our body works, and explains why proper digestion is so vital to our good health. It helps us to understand why it is the things that we consume that are the key to all of our health concerns.

This book explains in detail why it is the toxins that we consume that are the underlying cause of all disease, including cancer. It stresses the need for us to clean our body internally so that cancer cannot develop within us, and explains how we can go about doing that.

# *Introduction*

The development of cancer in the human body has always been a mystery. Nobody has ever really explained how cancer gets started, where it comes from, or why it strikes certain people and seems to leave others alone. In this book we will take a look at these questions, and come up with some very simple answers that might surprise you.

Many people today are searching for an alternative to conventional treatments for cancer. The only forms of treatment currently available that have any effect on cancer are chemotherapy and radiation, but as we all know, these deadly forms of treatment do not cure the disease, they only help to alleviate the symptoms. Also, these forms of treatment are often more harmful to your body than the disease they are trying to cure.

This book will take you through some of the reasons we have so much cancer in our society, and it will offer alternative methods by which your cancer can be defeated. Defeating cancer is not that difficult. All that is required is for you to get back in tune with

E.R. (Ron) Harder

Mother Nature, and follow a few simple steps that will help you to defeat this deadly disease.

When I say not that difficult, I mean that the concept is not that difficult. The difficult part is in changing our lifestyle from doing those things that have caused us to become ill, to doing those things that will help us to defeat this disease, and ensure a high level of health for ourselves.

This book starts with a discussion of digestion, how our intestines work, and why the operation of our intestines has so much to do with our overall health.

The following few chapters provide us with an understanding of WHY a disease such as cancer develops within us, and gives us some thoughts on how to prevent this from happening. The later chapters provide us with the SOLUTION that can help us to defeat any disease that we may have, including all forms of cancer.

Please note that this book is written in layman's language. There are no medical terms that are difficult to pronounce, and impossible to understand. It was written so that the general public could grasp the concept of good health from their own perspective.

Thank you for allowing me to share with you the information in this book. I sincerely hope that you will find this information useful, and that you will follow the suggestions given so that you can help your body to prevent any cancer from developing within you, and defeat any cancer that you may have, without taking chemo, without being subjected to radiation, and without having to undergo surgery.

# Chapter One

# The Process of Digestion

Digestion is one of the most important functions in our body, and one that most of us take for granted. It is an electrical process, and in order to explain it so that it can be properly understood, we have to look at it from an electrical point of view.

Absolutely everything in our entire universe is constructed of atoms (electrons, protons, and neutrons). This includes every element of nature; the wood in our trees, our water, our air, the food we eat, and the entire structure of the human body.

The molecular structure of the things that we consume have to be compatible with the electrical structure of our body in order for us to receive any nutritional value from them.

If what we consume is not electrically compatible with the matrix of our body, our body will not receive it as a nutrient but will receive it as a toxin. In other words, it will not nourish us, it will poison us.

## Electrical Configuration

We are very closely tied to the elements that surround us. We are made from the same components that are found in nature. To emphasize that, we should take a look and see what those components are.

Our body is constructed of the following elements. Oxygen, carbon, hydrogen, and nitrogen make up roughly 96% of the body's mass; and calcium, chlorine, iodine, iron, magnesium, phosphorus, potassium, sodium, and sulfur make up 3.9% of the balance. Trace elements make up the remaining 0.1%. All are required for life.

These are the same elements that we find in nature, and each of these has its own electrical matrix. The food that we eat has to be compatible with these electrical matrixes in order for us to receive any value from it.

If we change the molecular configuration of our food, we will change the way it interacts with our body. By changing the molecular configuration of any substance we change the number of electrons, protons and neutrons in this substance, and thereby change how it interacts with other substances.

Our universe depends on the interaction between all the different parts. It is held together by the electrical cohesion between all these parts, and it functions because of the compatibility between these same parts.

All of this cohesion can be looked at as electrical energy, and it can be said that all electrical energy is interrelated. In other words, everything is electrical energy, and electrical energy is in everything. This electrical energy becomes very important when we look at the process called digestion.

Our food is made up of electrical components, or molecules of different matter. Some of these particles of food will be electrically compatible with our bodies, and some will not. The parts of our food that are compatible will nourish our bodies, and the parts that are not compatible will not nourish us.

When we look at the process of food intake and waste elimination we can see that only a small fraction of the actual food we eat ever gets anywhere near the cells of our body, and the food that does find its way to our cells does so by following a complicated sequence of events. Most of our food goes through our digestive tract and ends up as waste material that is eventually eliminated.

**Gastrointestinal Functions**

Here is how the process of digestion works. We have some food in front of us that we are about to consume. Before we even put this food into our mouth, our senses tell us what that food is, and our body prepares itself to digest it. It takes different enzymes and gastric juices to digest different foods, and when our senses tell us what is coming, our body prepares the digestive tract for what we are about to eat.

When we put food into our mouth and chew it, we break it up into very small particles to allow the gastric juices and enzymes to begin their work of digestion. The more we chew our food the better this digestive process will be.

When we swallow our food, an action called peristalsis (wavelike contractions of the muscles in the wall of the gastrointestinal tract) propels food through our esophagus and transports it to the stomach. In the stomach, our food is mixed with enzymes and other digestive juices. Enzymes break down the carbohydrate, lipid, and protein molecules into smaller segments so that they can be absorbed through the lining of our intestines and used by our cells.

Several minutes after food enters the stomach, gentle rippling movements called mixing waves pass over the stomach. These occur about every twenty seconds. These waves churn up our food, mix it with gastric juices and enzymes, and reduce it to a thin liquid called chyme.

Every time these mixing waves pass over our stomach, a small portion of this chyme is pushed out of our stomach and enters the very first region of the small intestine.

Our small intestine is about one inch in diameter, about twenty-one feet long, and is divided into three segments. The first segment is the duodenum, the second segment is the jejunum, and the third segment is the ileum.

The duodenum, about ten inches long, absorbs mostly proteins and minerals. The jejunum, about eight feet long, absorbs mostly carbohydrates, proteins and water-soluble vitamins. The ileum, about twelve feet long, absorbs mostly bile salts, cholesterol, fat, and fat-soluble vitamins.

**Absorption**

About 90% of all the nutrients that are absorbed into our body are absorbed by the small intestine. The majority of the water the body needs is also absorbed by the small intestine.

All this absorption is made possible by something on the inner wall of our small intestine called "villi". Villi are one mm high, finger-like projections on the inside lining of the small intestine, and because there are thousands of these they vastly increase the surface area available for absorption and digestion.

The actual process of absorbing and digesting our food is very interesting, and it works like this. The enzymes and other digestive juices have been busy breaking down our food into tiny microscopic molecules that we can now absorb.

If the enzymes and digestive juices have done their job properly, the microscopic molecules of nutrients released from our food will be electrically attracted to the field of energy surrounding our small intestine.

This field of energy is very much like the field of energy surrounding an electromagnet, except that the magnetic/electrical field of energy surrounding the intestinal lining operates on a much smaller scale.

This field of energy will draw the microscopic molecules of nutrients through the porous intestinal lining and deposit them into the venules surrounding the small intestine.

These venules are actually very tiny veins, and when the molecules of nutrients are deposited into these venules, the nutrients are effectively released into the bloodstream.

At this point these tiny food particles would correctly be named "complex protein molecules", and as you can see, this process of absorbing nutrients through the lining of the small intestine is 100% electrical.

Your body will attempt to absorb the highest quality complex protein molecules that it can, and here is how this selection process works. Your body will seek out protein molecules that are electrically compatible with your matrix, and when it finds these, they will be absorbed. If your body cannot find protein molecules that are electrically compatible with your matrix, it will absorb the most compatible protein molecules that it can.

These complex protein molecules have now been carried through our veins, and have been pumped through our heart and into the veins and arteries of our lungs. In our lungs the blood picks up oxygen, and from there the complex protein molecules and the oxygen are passed into our arteries, and are now on their way to the capillaries of our body.

Capillaries are the tiny little blood vessels at the very ends of our arteries, and it is at this point that our protein molecules will be made available to the cells of our body. (See Chapter Eleven, Figure 6.)

Your protein molecules get to your cells as follows. The blood that is being pumped into your capillaries is made up of plasma and red blood cells, and it is the plasma portion of the blood that carries the oxygen and nutrients. As your capillaries become very small they wind their way between the cells of your body.

The capillary walls at this point are very thin, and this allows the plasma portion of your blood to be electrically drawn through these walls and enter into the region between your cells, carrying the oxygen and nutrients with it. This is accomplished by the same magnetic/electrical process that carried the molecules of nutrients through the small intestinal lining, which we discussed previously.

When the plasma enters the region between your cells it becomes known as interstitial fluid. Your interstitial fluid surrounds every cell in your body and very soon a protein molecule within this interstitial fluid will pass by one of your cells.

This little molecule is of opposite polarity to that of your cell, and when the molecule and the cell meet, the complex protein molecule will be electrically drawn into the cell, and the spent energy from the cell will be released back into the interstitial fluid.

New energy has been released into the cell, and spent energy, which is now waste material, has been released from the cell back into the interstitial fluid. (We will see in a later chapter how this interstitial fluid develops into lymphatic fluid that carries these spent energy particles away.)

Medically, this process of energy transfer from the interstitial fluid to your cell is called the sodium/potassium pump, and as you can see, this process is 100% electrical. If what you consume is not electrically compatible with your body, then the electrical energy transfer from your small intestinal lining to your bloodstream, from your capillaries to your interstitial fluid, and from your interstitial fluid to your cells, becomes distorted.

The greater this distortion, the less nutritional value you will receive from your food, and the more toxins and waste products you will build up within you.

This is basically how the process of digestion in your body works. It is more complicated than this because the digestive process also includes other organs such as the pancreas, liver, and gall bladder, but the main thing we are interested in here is the actual process of how the protein that you consume gets to the cells of your body.

The process described above should make it very clear just how important "Electrically Compatible Nutrition" is to your health and well-being. If you take a substance into your body that is not electrically compatible with your body's matrix, your body will not recognize it as food, but will consider it to be a toxin.

# *Chapter Two*

# **Our Food Supply**

When our forefathers first came to North America, they cut down small patches of trees and used the cleared land to grow their fruits, vegetables, and crops. The soil in which they grew these plants was full of natural bacteria, flora, and enzymes. For thousands of years Mother Nature had been putting nutrients back into the soil in the form of decayed vegetable and animal matter.

This decayed matter (natural fertilizer) replenished the soil with nutrients that continued to grow nutritional food that the people of that day depended upon to feed their families. This cycle of life and decay had been in existence for thousands of years, producing very rich soil that was alive with nutrients.

The farmers of that day understood that if you took from the soil you had to give back. Giving back meant using organic matter in the form of crop residue and other plant and animal waste material to place nutrients back into the soil.

It also meant leaving each parcel of soil alone every few growing seasons, to let minerals and bioorganic substances replenish themselves, and thereby re-establish the nutrients and trace elements necessary for healthy plant growth.

Our ancestors understood that healthy soil produces healthy crops, fruits, and vegetables, and that these in turn would provide them with the nourishment they needed for their own health.

The early part of the 20th century saw the introduction of modern agriculture and commercial farming. With this development, the emphasis in the production of food changed from the quality of the food being produced to the quantity. Getting the most out of that acre of land became priority one.

Letting the soil replenish itself with minerals and nutrients from natural sources became secondary because we now had other means to achieve this. Chemical fertilizers were introduced. If the production of your crop went down one year you simply dumped chemical fertilizer on it for the next growing season, and your production problems were solved.

Chemical fertilizers can substantially increase the yield of our product but they do so at a very high cost. Little did we know of the damage we were doing to our soil, and to ourselves.

## Our Healthy Soil

Let's look at our soil for a minute. Healthy soil moves continually in a natural cycle aided by oxygen, water, minerals, and decomposing animal and plant matter. All of these elements create life in the soil, which will be ongoing if not disturbed. We consider soil to be healthy if it works well, and nutrients continue to be available to the plants that grow in it.

Good soil consists of minerals and bioorganic substances and is a world of working microbes. For example, one gram of soil can contain over ten million microbial bacteria. Around the roots of a healthy growing plant a dense coating of soil may contain a population of 100 to 200 billion microbes, and most microbes in this environment will regenerate life in approximately thirty minutes.

Microbes live in colonies and are very mobile. In their life cycle, they develop tremendous metabolic activity and steadily improve the structure of the soil.

Some microbes excrete antibiotics. Others metabolize phosphorus and iron bonds, which are difficult to dilute efficiently without this microbial activity. This microbial activity is what gives the soil its earthy odor. Microbes also create two thirds of the soils carbons, attack cellulose, and mineralize nutrients.

There are other important life forces in the soil. These are mites, nematodes, centipedes, worms, and insects. All of these survive by eating plant and animal residue, eating each other, and producing excrements. When they die they leave waste products, which are very important in the formation of humus in the soil.

As you can see, good soil is very much alive. It is important to understand that if the soil is alive and healthy, the plants that grow in it will be healthy as well. They will be filled with nutrients and will have a natural resistance to disease. These healthy plants will provide us with the nutrients and enzymes that we need so that we can be healthy as well.

This healthy soil concept is the basic philosophy behind organic biological farming, which is what our ancestors unknowingly practiced.

## Modern Agriculture

Then along comes man with his modern agriculture and starts to destroy what nature has kept in balance for thousands of years. Because the emphasis has now changed from quality to quantity, the producer no longer has the incentive to produce top quality food products.

Farmers get paid by the pound for what they produce, whether it is for grains, tomatoes, cucumbers, potatoes, chickens, or beef. The major concern is now price per pound. You produce so many pounds, you get so many dollars. There is nothing in this equation about the quality of the food that is being produced.

Almost overnight the small farmer largely disappeared and was replaced by big agriculture organizations, which we now refer to as the food producing industry. This is when quantity over quality really became important and production got into high gear. The use of chemical fertilizers increased dramatically because now all that mattered was getting the most production that you could out of the land.

Then the food producing industry came up with some new ideas. They were not happy with how slow the chickens grow and how little milk the cows produced and decided to help things along. We now have chemicals being fed to the chickens that make them grow bigger, and in less time. We now use chemicals that help the cow produce more milk. We now have chemicals being dumped onto our soil to help the wheat grow larger kernels, and to give us a better "yield".

We also use chemicals to kill any bugs or insects that feed on our crops. We use chemicals in almost every line of food production to "help" Mother Nature along.

We have become even more arrogant and are now dumping industrial waste products onto our soil and calling it fertilizer. Many articles have been written on this subject, and it is too much to include here. If you would like more information on this topic kindly google "Hazardous waste in fertilizers", and you will be surprised at the amount of information that is available.

**Toxic Sprays**

There are other serious concerns that we should be aware of. It is not only the chemical fertilizers and hazardous industrial waste products that are being dumped onto our soil. We also spray our crops with tons and tons of pesticides. These are toxic chemicals that kill bugs and insects before they eat our crops.

Where does all this toxic material go? It runs off into our streams, rivers, and lakes, and takes a serious toll on wildlife. We now have hundreds of miles of streams and rivers that no longer support fish stocks. We have lakes that still support fish stocks, but some of these fish have been declared unfit for human consumption. And what are all these pesticides doing to the wildlife that lives beside the streams and rivers, and drinks this polluted water?

We have not talked about a wide range of topics such as the chemical content of our cleaning products, which we use and then pour down the drain. What about the chemicals that are used in hair spray and body deodorants? What about the chemical fertilizers we spray on our lawns that find their way into our water supplies?

I find it absolutely appalling to realize how far away we have gone from the way nature intended things to be. Yes, the chemical companies are to blame. Yes, the big food companies are to blame. And yes, our governments are to blame for bowing to the demands of these corporations, but we, the consumers, are also to blame for letting these people get away with all of this.

What we now have in our supermarkets is produce that has been altered to such a degree that it no longer provides us with the nutrition that we require. The vegetables have been grown using chemical and toxic fertilizers, and to make them more appealing, they are sprayed with wax.

The chickens are given chemical compounds to make them grow. The beef you buy is injected with all sorts of hormones. Very little of the food we now buy at the supermarket has any degree of nutritional value to it. It has been chemically altered to the point where even the taste is gone, but it looks good.

**Changed Electrical Structure**

In the previous chapter we discussed the process of digestion from an electrical point of view. We saw why the food we eat has to be electrically compatible with the matrix of our body before our body will accept it as food. Let us look for a moment at what happens when we dump chemicals and toxins onto our food supply, and how this affects digestion.

Absolutely everything we do to our food changes its molecular structure and thereby changes the way this food interfaces with our body. The fertilizers we use, the chemicals and toxins we put into our food, the pesticides we use to kill the insects, and the coloring we use, all change its electrical matrix.

Nature designed our food supply and the human body to be electrically compatible, but by using chemicals and toxins in the production of our food we have seriously altered this compatibility.

When we dump chemicals and toxic industrial waste products onto the soil, we kill the soil, period. We cannot expect the bacteria, microbes, and tiny life forces in the soil to survive when we dump lead, cadmium, arsenic and dioxins on them. We have just destroyed the cycle of life that has kept the plants healthy, and the soil alive.

Chemicals and toxic industrial waste products were not designed to be compatible with the electrical matrix of the human body. When we try to digest these things our body will reject them, store them in our colon, or maybe in our cells, or try to eliminate them. In other words, we are now depriving our body of nutrition, and we are poisoning ourselves.

Unfortunately, there is not one vegetable that is commercially grown in North America today that carries the same nutrients and enzymes that nourished our great grandparents. The nutrients that were in the soil one hundred years ago are long gone, and everything that grows from the soil is a direct reflection of what is in the soil.

One hundred years ago the fruits and vegetables that we ate carried with them the micro-bacteria, the enzymes and the nutrients that our bodies needed to survive. From an electrical compatibility point of view, the food at that time had the proper electrical matrix to be compatible with the requirements of our bodies.

**Genetically Modified Food**

Let me share with you another assault on our food supply, which has been going on for a number of years. Our engineers have decided that spraying our crops with herbicides and pesticides is too much trouble, and too expensive, and so they have taken it upon themselves to genetically alter the composition of our food crops so that spraying is no longer necessary.

What we now have is Genetically Modified Food. Instead of using sprays to control the infestation of bugs, insects, and disease, the new genetically modified plants have resistance to insects and disease already built in.

Here is how all this works. Each plant has a certain molecular makeup that makes it that type of plant. When we spray our crops with herbicides we are adding certain chemical substances to our crops which the bugs and insects find offensive. What we have sprayed onto our crops are chemicals that not only kill bugs and insects, they are also harmful to us.

Up until now, the farmer has had a choice as to whether or not he wants to use sprays on his crops, or if he wants to grow his crops without sprays. Genetically modified foods have been chemically altered to where the plant contains the molecular information for the plant, plus the molecular information for the substances that our scientists have bred into the plant.

These substances include various chemicals that combat disease, but they also include portions of the makeup of different plants. Hence the name "Frankenfoods". Allow me to explain.

Every plant is susceptible to a certain disease or to a certain insect. One type of bug will eat a stalk of wheat, but it may not touch soybeans for example. If you can determine what part of that soybean plant that particular bug finds offensive, and you were able to genetically alter the wheat plant to include this offensive substance, then in theory the bug would not attack the wheat plant either.

This is what our scientists have come up with. They are able to take portions of different plants that offer resistance to disease and insect attacks, and genetically breed these substances into plants that do not offer resistance to that particular disease or insect.

Therefore, what we now have may be a potato that is really part corn, part rose petal, or part birch tree. Our soybean may be made up of part canola, part wheat plant, and part alfalfa. What you think is a sunflower seed, may still look like a sunflower seed, but may in fact be something quite different.

The chemical composition of that kernel of wheat has been electrically altered so that this kernel of wheat, even though it may still look like a kernel of wheat, is no longer the kernel of wheat that used to be compatible with our electrical makeup. It has been genetically altered to be quite different from the food that Mother Nature designed for us.

The farmer no longer has a choice as to whether or not he wants to spray his crops, the decision has been made for him. The organic farmer, who wants to grow organic quality crops will not be able to if he uses seeds that have been genetically modified.

What makes all of this really scary is that no testing has been done to determine any effects this genetic engineering may have on human health. Nobody knows if this experiment will cause cancer, or brain damage, or deformed children, or heart disease, or anything else. The same as nobody knew of the deformities and disease that have been caused by the drugs that we were all told were safe to use during the past fifty years.

All of this genetic engineering has been going on for a lot of years. Our scientists, with the blessing and financial assistance of our government, have taken it upon themselves to test this genetically modified food on our population.

I find it difficult to imagine the arrogance of these people who have been using us as guinea pigs for their genetic experiments. This practice has been banned in parts of Europe, and I can only hope that our politicians will come to their senses and ban genetically modified food products in North America as well.

For anyone interested in the ongoing battle over GMO foods, Google "GMO myths and truths", and a lot of information will be made available.

**Organic Farming**

Now that I have painted a bleak picture of our food supply, let me say that there is a small bit of light at the end of that long dark tunnel. What I am referring to is going back to the way our ancestors grew their gardens one hundred years ago, and that is growing our food organically.

Organic food does not refer to a special type of food, but to the way in which food is grown and processed. Food is generally considered "organic" if it is produced using only natural additives, with no chemicals added.

Organic food production refers to a system of farming that maintains and replenishes the fertility of the soil. Organic foods are produced without the use of toxic pesticides or industrial waste products. Organic foods are processed to maintain the integrity of the food without artificial ingredients, preservatives, or irradiation.

The whole idea behind organic farming is to stay in tune with nature. This means building up and maintaining the cycle of life that is meant to be in our soil. It means putting natural nutrients back into the soil. It means keeping the soil alive and healthy.

Some of the objectives of organic food production are as follows:

a) To replenish and maintain long term fertility by providing optimal conditions for soil biological activity.

b) To produce viable quantities of high quality nutritious food and feed.

c) To encourage "closed cycle" farming systems using local resources and recycled nutrients.

d) To enhance ecological cycles within the food production system.

e) To maintain genetic diversity of the agricultural system and its surroundings, including protection of plants and wildlife habitat.

f) To sustain the land in a healthy condition for the enjoyment and use of future generations.

One group out of New York is working on a certification program that would seek complete compliance with the following standards.

a) Soils to be ecologically managed to conserve and recycle humus and nutrients by regular soil tests, crop rotation, cover crops, manures and composts. Naturally occurring organic matter, mineral and microbial fertilizers, not chemically fortified, may be used. Except for certain regulated substances, all synthetic fertilizers are prohibited.

b) Seeds and seedlings shall be, whenever possible, organically grown.

c) Weed control is to be by cropping practices such as timely planting and cultivation, cover crops, crop rotation, proper fertilizations and mulches. All chemical herbicides are prohibited.

d) Insect control to be provided by a healthy soil and farm ecosystem. Insect control must not harm the soil or farm ecosystem, or leave harmful residues. Approved methods include natural predators and parasites, mechanical removal, biological and botanical insecticides, attractants and traps. All synthetic insecticides and irradiation, a process that exposes food to radioactive material in order to kill bacteria, are prohibited.

e) Diseases are less of a problem when seeds and plants are selected for organic purity and grown in well-balanced fertile soil. Outbreaks to be treated by appropriate cultural practices, and natural non-toxic methods.

f)  Harvest and storage shall minimize insects and rodents without synthetic fumigants, insecticides, preservatives, irradiation or prohibited substances.

g)  Processing and packaging to be without any synthetic substances such as artificial flavors, artificial colors, preservatives, antibiotics, and irradiation.

The above objectives and standards give us a very good description of what organic farming is intended to be. As you can see, it is all about producing our food in such a manner as to stay in harmony with nature.

Organic farming has come a long way in North America. Sales of organic food is now in the many billions of dollars a year and doing well, and the market is enjoying a growth rate of 10% a year.

As with everything else in a free market economy, supply and demand determines the success of any venture, and organic farming is no different. If we want this industry to grow and provide healthy food for ourselves and for our family, it is up to us to support it. We can do our part by supporting our local organic farmer, and eating only those food products that we know to be organic, or as close to organic as possible.

You may think that organic food costs more, but that is not really the case. Prices of organic food reflect many of the same costs as conventional food in terms of growing, harvesting, transportation, and storage.

However, organically produced foods must meet stricter regulations governing all these steps, and so the process is often more labor and management intensive. Also, organic farming tends to be on a smaller scale. All these combined may increase the cost slightly.

Here is one other point to consider. If all the indirect costs of conventional food production, not associated with organic food production, were taken into account, organic food production costs would be the same as, or more likely, less than the cost of conventional production.

Conventional food production costs should include the cleanup of polluted water, replacement of eroded soils, the cost of health care for farmers and their workers, and the cost of restoring fish habitat etc.

As you can see, there are groups of concerned citizens who are working to get the quality of our food supply back to the standards we once enjoyed. We have to realize that our commercially grown food supply is in bad shape, and that it will be up to us to change it.

One group that is working hard on the problem of food quality is the Organic Farmers Marketing Association (OFMA). They are involved in a battle to keep the big corporate agriculture corporations out of the organic food business, a situation that would seriously dilute the standards of organic farming.

They can be reached on their web site at www.iquest. net/ofma. It is up to everyone to support the organic farming organizations in their fight for their right to produce healthy, nutritious food.

In this chapter we discussed the quality of our food supply, and how it got that way. In a later chapter we will look in detail at how the quality of our food affects our health, and what we can do to help this situation.

# Chapter Three

# The Start of Disease

It has been said that "You Are What You Eat", and it would seem that truer words were never spoken. The state of your health is directly proportional to the quality of the food you eat and the quality of the liquids you drink, and in this chapter we will take a look at why this is so. We will start with the digestive tract and see what happens to the food you eat as it is carried along.

In the first chapter we followed the process of digestion as far as the small intestine, and we saw how the usable nutrients were absorbed through the wall of the small intestine, and how they were made available to the cells of your body. In this chapter we will focus on what happens to the food that is not absorbed.

## The Colon

The food that is not utilized by our body passes through the small intestine and is moved along to the large intestine, also known as the colon. To help us understand what happens in the colon we will take a look at what the colon is and how it works.

If you look at Figure 1 you will see a drawing of a normal colon. In an average person, the colon is about five feet long and two and a half inches in diameter. It extends from the ileum (exit of the small intestine) to the anus, and is sectioned into four individual regions. These regions are the cecum, the colon, the rectum, and the anal canal.

The movement of undigested food material is from the small intestine, through the ileum, and into the cecum. At this point, if there are too many toxins in this material, the toxins will be stored in the appendix until such time as the colon is able to eliminate them from your body.

Your undigested waste material moves from the cecum upwards through the ascending colon, then from the right side of your body to the left side through the transverse colon, and then down through the descending colon, through the sigmoid colon, and on to the rectum where it is stored until it is eliminated.

Two important things happen to this waste material as it passes from the cecum to the rectum. First of all, the last stage of digestion occurs in the colon, and any remaining usable nutrients are extracted from the waste material and sent to different regions of your body.

Also, if your body is in need of more water, it will also extract this from the waste material that is in the colon before it is eliminated.

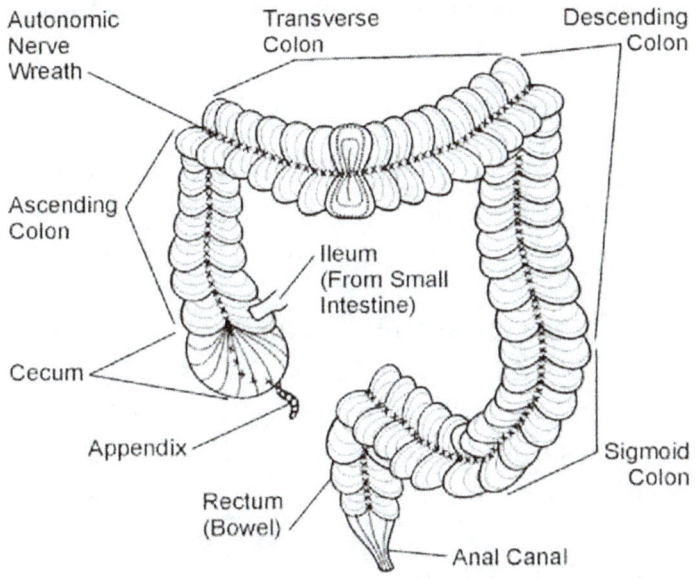

Figure 1. Normal Colon

It normally takes up to three hours for the remaining nutrients to be removed, and the available water to be extracted. After this period of time the waste material will have become semi-solid, and will then become known as feces.

There are two major problems that can occur as a result of either excess or insufficient water in the colon, and they are diarrhea and constipation. Diarrhea results from decreased water absorption in the intestines, or by waste material passing through the colon too quickly for the water to be absorbed, and either of these will make the chyme very liquid. This can sometimes be caused by stress, and can result in dehydration.

The other major problem is constipation, and this occurs when there is either insufficient water content in the waste material, or there is considerable water absorption from the material that is in the colon.

Constipation can also result from feces remaining in the colon for an extended period of time because of improper bowel habits, consuming the wrong kinds of foods, insufficient fiber in the diet, insufficient fluid intake, or lack of exercise.

**Proper Nourishment**

Before we continue with our discussion of the colon I would like to mention that your body can only perform in relation to the quality of the nutrition that it receives. This is to say, that if you do not provide your body with nourishing food, you cannot expect it to be healthy and disease free, and to be able to perform to its maximum potential.

If you do not consume quality nutrition, your body will not receive the nutrients that it needs to allow it to perform the functions it was intended to perform. In a previous chapter we had a look at the chemicals and waste products that are in your commercially grown food, and it does not surprise me at all that a lot of us have some health issues.

## Colon Diseases

If you do not provide your body with proper nutrition, you can expect three very common conditions to occur. You can develop a stricture in your colon, you can develop a ballooned colon, or you can develop diverticula pockets in the wall of your colon. These three conditions are shown in Figure 2.

It is known that different diets cause one or more of these conditions to occur in the colon, but it is not known which type of diet causes which disease. Whatever the specific cause, disease because of improper diet will weaken your colon wall, and one or more of the conditions mentioned above can occur.

The first of these conditions is a stricture, and when a stricture occurs, the colon is almost entirely prevented from passing the waste material along for elimination.

As you can see in Figure 2, when a stricture occurs, the colon diameter is reduced to just a fraction of its normal size. This will cause the waste material in the colon to back up, and that will put tremendous pressure on the colon wall at the point before the stricture.

The second of these conditions is a ballooned colon. The colon wall is very elastic and has been known to expand to many times its normal diameter. When ballooning occurs in front of a stricture, only a small portion of the material from this ballooned colon will be passed along for elimination. The majority of it will remain in the colon where it will decay and become toxic because of all the bacteria that develops in it.

The third of these conditions is diverticulosis. If the body signals that waste removal is necessary and you do not allow this waste removal to occur, this material will back up into your colon. Your colon wall will stretch, and if the pressure is too severe, a small pocket may develop in the side of your colon (a rupture), and this will form into what is known as a diverticula pocket.

In a very short period of time this diverticula pocket will become filled with waste material, and because the waste material inside this pocket is no longer in the main elimination path, this waste material will not be removed through normal elimination processes. It will decay and become toxic. (You can have numerous diverticula pockets in your colon and not be aware of it until your colon shows signs of disease.)

The ballooning condition of the colon and the diverticulosis will become particularly severe in a situation where constipation is present. The solid or semi-solid nature of the waste material in this situation will almost guarantee that this material will remain in these pockets, and will become diseased.

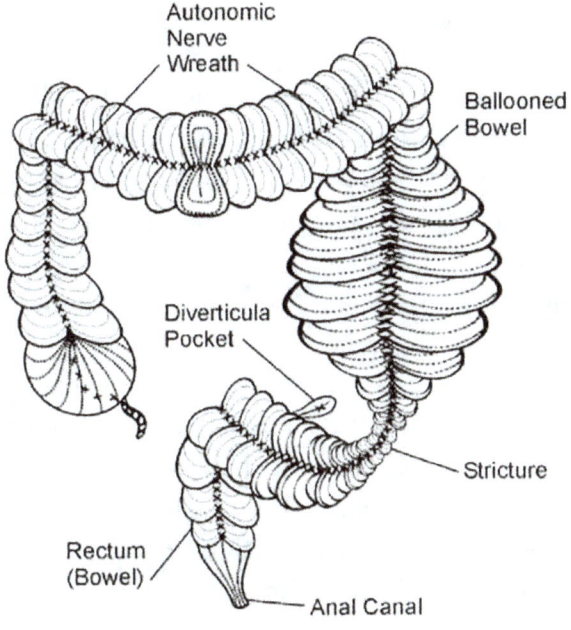

Figure 2. Abdominal Colon

Most people have no idea that these conditions are occurring in their colon because they do not notice anything other than perhaps a slight discomfort from time to time. These conditions develop very slowly and it could be years before you have any indication that anything is wrong.

**The Autonomic Nervous System**

There is one item indicated in Figures 1 and 2 that we have not yet discussed and that is the Autonomic Nerve Wreath (ANW). As shown, the ANW is attached to and runs along the entire length and along both sides of the colon, starting at the cecum and ending at the anal canal. Let's look at what this is so we can understand its function.

The Autonomic Nerve Wreath is part of the Autonomic Nervous System (ANS), which in turn is part of your Central Nervous System (CNS). These two nervous systems are both controlled by the brain, and they each perform different functions.

The central nervous system controls the senses (vision, hearing, taste, smell, and touch) and all skeletal muscle functions, which is to say it controls all physical movement of your body.

The Autonomic Nervous System controls smooth muscle fiber, cardiac muscle fiber, and the function of the organs and glands. In other words, all involuntary actions in your body.

Let me expand on that a little. You do not consciously have to tell your heart to beat or your liver to function. You do not have to tell your individual organs and glands to function, your ANS does that for you. This is because the electrical stimulation that they require to function properly is provided by the ANS.

The portion of the ANS that we are concerned with here is the motor division, also called the output portion of the ANS. It is called the output portion because the ANS generates autonomic nerve fibers (signals) that are sent to the various portions of your body that are controlled by the ANS. In general, these nerve fibers stimulate various organs to start or increase activity (excitation), or they can stimulate the organs to decrease activity (inhibition).

Most body structures receive both excitation and inhibition signals from the ANS, and how the structures and organs respond depends on the motor instruction received.

If you look at Figure 3, you will see a drawing of the colon with a number of other body parts also indicated in the drawing. The body parts indicated are connected via nerve fibers to the colon at the locations indicated.

For example, the dot indicated as being the pancreas is connected via nerve fibers, through the ANS, to the pancreas. The dot indicated as being the heart is connected via nerve fibers, through the ANS, to the heart.

What this indicates is that there is a direct correlation between your colon and all the other parts of your body that are controlled by the ANS. The colon receives nerve impulses FROM these other locations, and it also sends nerve impulses TO these other locations, via the ANS.

If you take another look at Figure 2 you can see the disease conditions that we discussed earlier. The portions of the colon that are ballooned, or have diverticula pockets formed on it, will have decaying waste material inside it and will very likely be toxic and full of bacteria.

This toxic material will have a direct impact on the health of the colon wall. The autonomic nerve wreath is attached to the colon wall and is part of the ANS. Therefore, anything that affects one will affect the other. This means that the health of the colon will have a direct impact on the type of stimulation that the ANW sends out.

Now, if the wall of the colon has become diseased because of the toxic material inside it, it cannot send out a STIMULATING nerve impulse, but can only send out an INHIBITING nerve impulse instead.

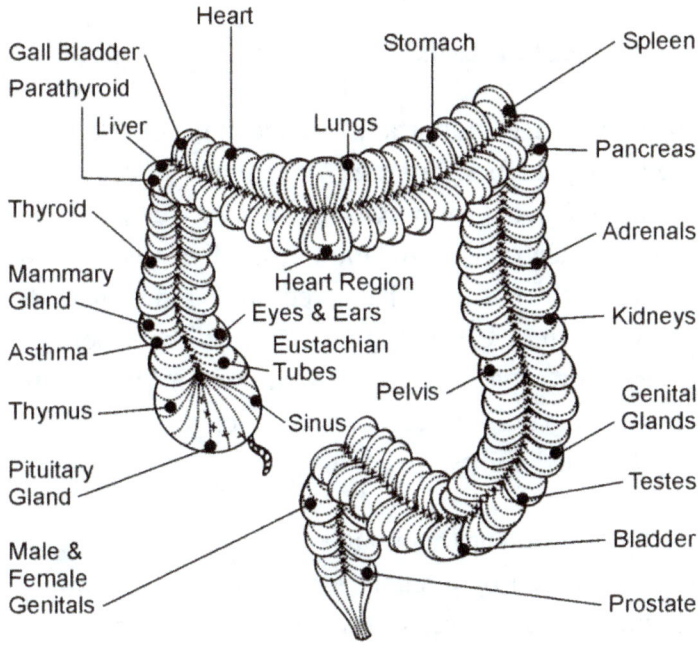

Figure 3. Autonomic Nerve Fiber Centers

To take this a little further, if the infected portion of your colon is in the location that has nerve impulses going to your heart, then your heart can only receive INHIBITING electrical nerve impulses instead of STIMULATING nerve impulses from the ANW.

Any portion of your colon that has a disease condition affecting it will send an INHIBITING nerve impulse to the body part corresponding to it.

## Two Essential Items

It is extremely important to understand that all the cells in your body require two things in order for them to remain healthy. One is nutrition (fuel), and the other is electrical stimulation. Your digestive system provides the nutrition that is required, and your ANS provides the electrical stimulation. Without both of these, any organ, gland, or tissue within your body will become diseased, and will no longer function to its designed ability.

If the electrical nerve impulses received from the ANS are decreased by a small degree, the corresponding tissue will decrease its function by the same small degree. If your pancreas is receiving sufficient nutrition but is receiving INHIBITING electrical impulses from the ANS, your pancreas will decrease in efficiency.

The action of the ANW and its direct link to the ANS is what makes your colon such a vital part of your body. The health of your colon has a direct effect on the health of any part of your body that the ANS is attached to, which is most of it.

This brings us to one very important point. A medical condition you may have in your kidneys, for example, may not be a problem with your kidneys at all. It could very well be, and probably is, a diseased condition in the corresponding region of your colon.

There have been many documented cases where the underlying cause of a problem with an organ has ultimately been traced back to the corresponding region of the colon, and when we examine the relationship between the affected organ and the colon, we can understand why this would be so.

These cases may not have been documented by your local family doctor, but they have been documented by persons practicing other forms of medicine.

**Missed Diagnosis**

You may be wondering why your family doctor might not be able to pick up on this relationship between disease and the colon, and the answer is very simple. In most cases, your doctor is only knowledgeable on the things that he has been taught in medical school, and dietary health may not be very high on the instructor's agenda. He is much more concerned with teaching those things that are included in the curriculum, like drugs, for example.

Also, most doctors are taught to diagnose disease by looking at the symptoms of any problem that you may have, so if the symptoms tell your doctor that you have a malfunction in your kidneys, the colon would likely be the last place your doctor would look.

## Your Weakest Link

You may have asked yourself why disease strikes one portion of your body and not another, and there are two parts to the answer. First of all, if a toxic element is allowed to invade your body, it will affect the weakest organ or tissue first.

Second, if a toxic condition in your colon is allowing an INHIBITING nerve impulse instead of a STIMULATING nerve impulse to be transmitted, then that organ or tissue the particular portion of the colon corresponds to will become weak, and will be the first body part to be affected by invading toxic particles.

As you can see from the above, the colon is responsible for a large number of your body's illnesses. This includes all types of illnesses ranging from diabetes, to asthma, to heart disease, to vision problems, and it is especially applicable to cancer.

Cancer can very easily develop throughout your body as a result of various body parts receiving INHIBITING nerve impulses in place of STIMULATING nerve impulses from your Autonomic Nervous System.

## Colon Cancer

We have seen how a toxic condition in your colon can generate a disease condition in a corresponding part of your body, but we have not looked at what these toxins can do to the colon itself.

I mentioned under Colon Diseases that there were three very common conditions that can occur in your colon, and one of these is the formation of diverticula pockets. Diverticula pockets may be present in your body for years before you get any indication of it, and the indication that you do get may not be very pleasant.

These pockets are filled with toxins that sit there and ferment, and in a lot of cases they will develop into a very common disease known as colon cancer. The big "C" word in medicine.

These pockets have in all likelihood been filled with a toxic substance for some period of time, and under those conditions you really could not expect your colon to remain healthy forever.

Cancer throughout your body in all its various forms has become the number two killer in North America, and to give you an idea of how serious a problem cancer really is, let me state one very important statistic that comes from the medical community.

Ten years ago, it was estimated that one out of every three people in North America would develop cancer at some point during their lifetime. Five years ago that estimate was revised to where one out of every two people was expected to develop cancer. That has been revised again. The latest estimate says that up to 100% of the population is expected to develop cancer at some point during their lifetime.

In other words, I am being told that I will develop cancer, and if nothing else gets me first, cancer probably will. Pretty scary stuff for most of us. And, what most of us don't realize is that this cancer is directly or indirectly being caused by a toxic colon, which is being made toxic by the chemically poisoned items that we consume.

## The Development Of Cancer

Here is some information that may surprise you. We all have from 1,000 to 100,000 cancer cells floating around in our body at any given time. These cancer cells are meant to be there, and in a healthy person they do not cause a problem.

They serve a definite purpose, and this purpose is to devour toxic waste material that they find anywhere in your body. In other words, **the development of cancer in your body is a protective response**.

Your body manufactures cancer cells in an effort to clean up the toxic waste material that you have accumulated within you. Where does this toxic waste material come from? Some of it comes from the water that you drink, some of it comes from the air that you breathe, but most of it comes from the food that you eat.

Your body will try to protect itself from disease by developing cancer cells that devour toxic waste material and storing this toxic material until such time as it is able to eliminate it. If you accumulate a large number of toxins, or if you accumulate toxins faster than you can eliminate them, you will require a large number of cancer cells to store these toxins.

Your body will develop all the cancer cells that it needs to store the toxins that accumulate within you. If you keep putting toxins into your body faster than you can eliminate them, the number of cancer cells will continue to grow. These cancer cells will accumulate in pockets where the toxins are located, and you will then develop what is known as a tumor.

A tumor will develop first wherever you have the largest accumulation of toxins, whether that is in your colon, your kidneys, in your lymphatic system, or anywhere else that toxins accumulate.

E.R. (Ron) Harder

There are two kinds of tumors; benign tumors that grow and stay in the area in which they originate, and malignant tumors, whose cells detach themselves from the original tumor and spread to different parts of your body through the blood or lymphatic system, and establish themselves as cancer in other weakened portions of your body.

By its very nature, by the time a malignant tumor ever gets large enough to be detected, it has already spread to other parts of your body. When this tumor is then detected and radiation treatment is undertaken, the radiation is usually only directed at the portion of your body that shows signs of cancer growth. This allows the cancer cells that have detached themselves from the main growth to accumulate in other regions of your body that are not being treated.

If you continue to consume toxins, it could take some time for this new accumulation to develop to the point of being detectable, and this is a large reason why tumors develop in other parts of your body years after the initial radiation treatments have been completed for your original cancer.

Here is some more information that may surprise you. All tumorous cancer in your body is the same. The tumor that you may have in your stomach is caused by the same cancer cells as the tumor that you may have in other parts of your body.

Our medical community would have us believe that there are many different types of cancer, but that is not so. The only difference is that the tumor has developed in one part of your body instead of another. It makes no difference in what part of your body toxins accumulate, your cancer cells will go wherever you have the largest accumulation of toxins.

## Heredity

While we are on the topic of how disease is generated in our bodies, I would like to say a few words about how various diseases are passed on to our offspring. Some people believe that certain diseases run in their family. They believe that if their mother had kidney problems, that they will have kidney problems as well, or because their father had a bad heart that they will also have a bad heart.

They look at this as certain disease conditions being hereditary in their family. Disease can and does get passed along to future generations, but heredity has nothing to do with it.

Heredity is defined as "The transmission of characteristics from parent to offspring by means of genes". This refers to passing on family traits that have to do with physical characteristics such as height, body type, hair color etc. It has nothing to do with passing on disease. If your mother had red hair, it is likely that you will also have red hair.

E.R. (Ron) Harder

Just because cancer or heart disease may have been a serious problem in your family does not mean that it will be a problem for you. Let me try to explain.

In a perfect world we would all be created equal. In other words, we would all be in perfect health when we were born. Our bones would all have formed properly, our hearts would all be strong, we would all have the right number of fingers and toes, and we would all have the same opportunity to lead normal, healthy lives. However, this is not always the case.

One hundred years ago our ancestors did not have junk food. There were no chips, no pop, and no fast foods. A snack to them was eating an apple, or maybe munching on a carrot they had just picked from the garden. Because of the quality of the food they ate they were generally a lot healthier and stronger than we are.

Diseases like cancer were unheard of until someone was past middle age. Today, we have babies being born who already have cancer, and there is a very good reason for this.

I don't think anybody can dispute that the health of a fetus is directly tied to the health of the mother, and this is because whatever the mother consumes will be passed on to the fetus. The unborn baby does not have a choice about the quality of the nutrition that it receives.

We have all heard of babies being born with a drug dependency. This is because the mother was on cocaine, or heroin, or some other drug while she was pregnant with the child. The health of the baby is a direct reflection of the health of the mother during pregnancy.

The same principle also applies during the child's infancy. Whatever Mom and Dad eat is what the toddler eats. If the parents eat food that does not provide the proper nourishment for healthy growth, how can you expect the child to grow up strong and healthy?

This is now a very serious problem because we have raised a generation of junk food addicts. Combine that with all the toxins being put into our commercial food, and a lot of our young people really do not have a very good chance at good health.

What does all this have to do with heredity? Just this. The health of the children is closely tied to the health of the parents, but it has nothing to do with heredity, it has everything to do with the same dietary habits.

If the parents are hooked on junk food, it is very likely that the children will be hooked on junk food as well. If the mother is overweight, and if the daughter has the same diet, then it is very likely that the daughter will also be overweight.

We can take this one step further. If a parent has a particular diet, and that diet has caused a heart condition to occur, then the child with the same diet will very likely develop a heart condition as well. Or, if a parent has a diet that has caused cancer, and the child has the same diet, then cancer is also likely to occur in the child. Heredity has nothing to do with it.

This process of passing on disease conditions to our offspring can easily be broken by changing our own, and our children's diet. We can break this cycle of passing on disease conditions to our children by educating them, and ourselves, about the value and benefits of eating proper nutritional food.

In this chapter we looked at how and why most diseases, especially cancer, originate in our body, and in a later chapter we will take a look at what we can do to prevent cancer from occurring, how we can defeat any cancer that we may have, and how we can keep our body in good health.

# Chapter Four

# Iridology

How can you find out whether or not you have waste products building up in your colon if your local health care professional is not able to tell you? There is a way.

For thousands of years the Orientals have known that a person's diet has a direct and very significant effect on their health. Through research and careful observation they were able to develop a science that would allow them to diagnose almost any disease condition in the body by looking at the iris of the eye. Yes, that's right, the iris of the eye.

This science has developed into what we now call "Iridology", which has been defined as "The science and practice of determining one's health through the examination of the iris of the eye".

Iridology has been practiced in North America since the early 1900s. It never really caught on in the medical community because, first of all, the medical community does not consider it to be an exact science, and second, it falls into the category of preventive medicine instead of corrective medicine.

It can and has been used very successfully to determine various potential health problems in the body BEFORE they occur. Our modern medical practitioners don't seem to be very interested in preventive medicine and in most cases only deal with a disease condition after the disease has become obvious.

Let me explain very briefly how Iridology works. The iris of the eye is normally constructed of unique fibers and tissues that are either medium blue or medium brown in color. Also, the texture of a normal iris is opaque and shows very little definition. Any changes to this, such as dark markings, dark lines, variations in color, etc., indicate that all is not well with a particular portion of your body.

The connection between the iris and the rest of your body is made through the brain and the autonomic nervous system (ANS), much the same way as the connection to your colon is made. The iris (the colored part of the eye) is like a map, in that different regions of the iris represent different regions of your body. No two irises are exactly alike, because no two bodies are exactly alike when it comes to their level of health.

If you look at Figure 4 for a moment you will see an Iridology Chart of the left eye. Iridology Charts normally indicate both the left and the right eye, but for our purposes looking at one eye will be sufficient.

The letters A to L, indicated on the outside of the iris, represent general areas within the iris. These general areas start at the edge of the iris and extend halfway toward the pupil.

Area A, for example, includes all of area 13, which is made up from the sensory, inherent mental, equilibrium, and medulla sections of the physiological brain. Area E, the upper abdomen, would have within it the spleen, ovary-testes, and general upper abdomen.

A trained Iridologist can examine your eyes and determine the state of your health very accurately. He does this by looking for abnormal markings in your iris and noting the precise location of these markings.

The location, the shape, the size, and the color of the markings will tell the trained Iridologist where a problem is developing, what type of problem it is, and how serious it is.

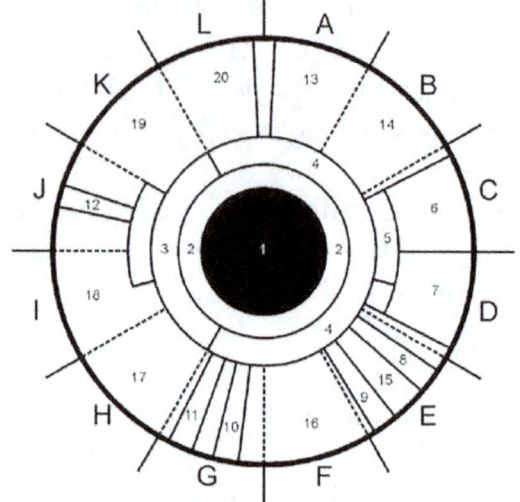

Figure 4. Iridology Chart Showing Left Iris

A - Physiological Brain
B - Neck
C - Lung
□ - Thorax
E - Upper Abdomen
F - Lower Abdomen
G - Pelvic
H - Lower Back
I - Upper Back
J - Throat
K - Face
L - Psychological Brain
1 - Pupil
2 - Stomach
3 - Small Intestine
4 - Colon
5 - Heart
6 - Left Lung
7 - Thorax
8 - Spleen
9 - Ovary - Testes
10 - Kidney
11 - Vagina
12 - Thyroid

13 - Sensory
  Inherent Mental
  Equilibrium
  Medulla
14 - Ear
  Neck
  Shoulder
15 -Abdomen
16 - Pelvis
  Groin
  Left Leg
17 -Bladder
  Lower Back
18 - Upper Back
  Esophagus
19 - Left Eye
  Upper Jaw
  Nose
  Tongue
20 - Sensory
  Speech
  Mental Ability

Abnormal conditions in your heart, in your lungs, or in any other regions of your body are indicated in your iris, and you will know of an upcoming medical problem long before you ever develop any symptoms. This will allow you to take preventive measures and hopefully avoid any serious health problems.

One of the very first things a trained Iridologist will look for in your eyes is the condition of your colon. In your left eye the colon is indicated in area number 4 and it is easy to see a stricture, a ballooned colon, or a toxic condition in your colon simply by studying this area.

Iridology is a complete science all by itself and we do not have the space in this book to cover this topic in any detail. If you wish to learn more about this science you can obtain a copy of a book entitled *The Science and Practice of Iridology - Volume 1,* by Dr. Bernard Jensen.

Dr. Jensen had a medical practice in California. He passed away in February of 2001, but while he was alive he was considered to be the foremost North American authority on the subject of Iridology. The books he has written on the subject are used in many schools as training texts. The book mentioned above and other material can be obtained by doing a book title search on Google.

# Chapter Five

## Dental Health

When we think of dental health the first thing that comes to mind is having a toothache, followed by having bad breath, and perhaps having dental cavities. Of these three, having a cavity is the most serious.

A toothache is usually the first sign of tooth decay and can normally be taken care of by applying a bonded sealer to your teeth to prevent further decay. Bad breath can be taken care of by cleaning your teeth, but having a cavity filled to prevent further decay is much more serious.

### Dental Amalgam

In the event you do have a cavity in one or more of your teeth you will have to have that cavity filled with something. For a lot of years a common filling material used was a substance called Dental Amalgam. Amalgam is a material that is composed of mercury, in combination with silver, tin, copper and zinc. The silver, tin, copper and zinc make up about

50% of the amalgam, and mercury, an extremely toxic metal, makes up the other 50%.

In the mid 1980s people became very concerned about the dangers of mercury, especially the mercury used in dental fillings. Reports started coming in about all kinds of negative effects this mercury filling material was having on people, and several detailed studies were completed to find out the effects on health.

It is now firmly believed that mercury in the amalgam dental filling material is responsible for a wide range of health problems including Alzheimer's, dizziness, headaches, chronic fatigue syndrome, learning disabilities, memory loss, blurred vision, heart problems, weakened immune system, asthma, fatigue, depression, cramps, kidney damage, thyroid gland disturbance, and many more.

**It is now known that Mercury is more poisonous than arsenic and is also listed as a carcinogenic (cancer causing) material**. If you have dental fillings in your mouth that have been there for a while, chances are they are made from some form of amalgam.

In 1985 the International Academy of Oral Medicine and Toxicology (IAOMT) reviewed the transcript of the National Institute of Dental Research (NIDR) workshop on the biocompatibility of Metals in

Dentistry, and concluded that there was reasonable doubt about the safety of dental amalgam. They recommended that the use of mercury in fillings be discontinued until such time as the safety of mercury in amalgam could be determined. This recommendation was never followed.

Shortly after this, the American Dental Association (ADA) and the Canadian Dental Association (CDA) both published articles stating that the use of dental amalgam was safe for filling material. This was done without any scientific research showing the safety of amalgam.

Since most dentists in North America rely on information and guidelines from the ADA and the CDA, it is extremely important that any information passed on by these organizations be honest and accurate, especially when it concerns public health.

When asked if mercury was safe when used in amalgam, the ADA replied that when mercury is combined with other metals in forming dental amalgam, it reacts with them to form a safe, inactive substance.

This has been proven not to be true. Tests have confirmed that mercury is released from the dental amalgam in the form of mercury vapor, especially when chewing food, brushing your teeth, or when drinking a hot liquid. This mercury vapor is then absorbed through the lungs into the bloodstream and distributed throughout the body.

## Scientific Testing

The half-life of mercury in humans is approximately seventy days. Because of this, daily doses of mercury will cause a significant amount to be accumulated over time. To prove this theory, tests were done using pregnant sheep that had amalgam placed into their molars.

Radioactivity measurements were used to determine the presence and the amount of mercury building up in their bodies from these amalgam fillings. The design of this experiment was specifically for mercury from amalgams, and eliminated any other possible mercury source. The findings were very disturbing and are listed here.

Day three: Mercury found in maternal and fetal blood, urine, and feces.

Day sixteen: Mercury levels highest in maternal kidney, liver, GI tract, and thyroid. Fetal levels highest in pituitary, liver, kidney, and placenta.

Day thirty-three: Most fetal tissues had higher levels of mercury than maternal tissues, especially the liver, epiphytical bone, bile, bone marrow, blood, and brain.

Day seventy-three: Tests showed that mercury levels in the maternal kidneys, liver, pancreas, pituitary glands, urine, bile, brain, and thyroid were still rising.

These laboratory tests show that mercury does accumulate in your body from the amalgam material used for tooth fillings. Mercury is a heavy metal and is considered unsafe in any amount.

## Mercury Poisoning

There are reported instances where children have suffered severe effects shortly after having fillings installed or replaced in their teeth. Some of these effects are severe enough so that the child is no longer able to walk and cannot think clearly.

Sudden symptoms after having fillings placed in your child's teeth, such as allergies, arthritis, chronic fatigue, depression etc., could be caused by amalgam, and should be checked.

It is estimated that as much as 20% of the population is affected by mercury in amalgam. It has also been reported that 10 million amalgam fillings are placed each year in the US. This amounts to several tons of mercury being used each year in dentistry.

There are several countries that have either partially or completely banned the use of mercury in fillings.

These include Germany, Sweden, Norway, and Austria.

If you suspect that you may have amalgam fillings, or if you have symptoms such as the ones mentioned that you do not know the cause of, it might be a good idea to have any amalgam fillings replaced.

Your dentist may tell you that this is not necessary, but you are ultimately responsible for your own health, and for your own health decisions. Your dentist is not your health care professional, and he may have no idea of the damage that can be caused by the amalgam fillings that he puts into your teeth.

As a point of interest, if you are having fillings placed into your teeth in Canada, the substance that your dentist will use will be amalgam. Having a non-toxic compound placed into your teeth is an extra, and you may have to pay out-of-pocket for any upgraded type of material.

**Fluoride**

Another serious issue that has to do with dental health is the use of fluoride. Fluoride is present in many things, including drinking water and toothpaste. The use of fluoride is now a very contentious issue and we should go back a ways and see how all this controversy over fluoride got started.

For many years now, a battle has been going on over whether fluoride should or should not be added to drinking water. As early as 1961, fluoride was exposed as a lethal poison in the US water supply. Those who support its use say that fluoride occurs naturally, and helps develop and maintain strong bones and teeth.

Opponents to the use of fluoride say that when fluoridated water is consumed, toxic levels of fluorine, the poisonous substance of fluoride, builds up in the body and causes severe harm to bone tissue and to teeth. It also does severe damage to your immune system.

In the early part of this century fluoride was recognized as a dominant industrial pollutant. It is very common in the earth's crust and because of that, whenever we mine raw materials, we bring up a lot of it. It is emitted from iron and steel manufacturing operations, from aluminum, copper, lead, and zinc manufacturing operations, and is a by-product of fertilizer.

**Opportunity Knocks**

Nobody really knew what to do with this toxic material, and then, simply through circumstance, somebody came up with an ingenious plan. It was reported that there were some areas in the United States where there were relatively high levels of natural fluoride in the drinking water supply, and that there appeared to be lower rates of dental cavities in those areas.

This was looked upon by the concerned industrial interests as a golden opportunity, and they seized it. Turn the public image of fluoride around from being an industrial pollutant to being something that helps prevent cavities, and your problem about toxic waste disposal is solved.

The bottom line, of course, was this. Instead of having it cost a pile of money to dispose of this toxic waste material, some manufacturing industries were now making money by selling this toxic by-product to water companies as something that will help to prevent cavities by putting it into your drinking water.

To give you an example of the money involved, it is estimated that it would cost up to $8,000 US per ton to dispose of this hazardous waste. At a rate of emissions into the air of 155,000 tons per year, in addition to an estimated 500,000 tons of emissions into lakes, oceans, and rivers, it is very clear that industry saves billions of dollars annually in toxic waste disposal. You can bet your bottom dollar they were not going to let this opportunity pass them by.

The issue of fluoride was never about saving children's teeth, it was always about an industry- backed program to dispose of toxic waste. It is now about big business, mega dollars, dirty politics, and about protecting a long-standing public health policy, which falsely claims that fluoridation is safe and effective in preventing cavities.

This fictitious concept is being kept alive by the persecution of reputable scientists, conformity and fear. In other words, play ball or lose your job.

It is interesting to note that today, more than half the cities in the US fluoridate their water supplies, and in many states it is required. Because of this, every processed food product or beverage prepared in a fluoridated community contains fluoride, and it is simply impossible to avoid this toxic substance in those products. Even some natural spring water that comes from a fluoridated community may have fluoride listed as one of its ingredients.

**Two Types Of Fluoride**

It is important to understand that there are two different types of fluoride. The naturally occurring form of fluoride, calcium fluoride, is not toxic, but this form of fluoride is not used to fluoridate water, and is not used in toothpaste.

The salts used to fluoridate your water supply, sodium fluoride and fluorosalicic acid, are industrial by-products that are so notoriously toxic that they are used in rat poison and insecticides. This is the fluoride that is used in your water supply, and when we refer to fluoride in the rest of this chapter we are referring to sodium fluoride and fluorosalicic acid.

Fluoride is an acute toxin with a rating slightly higher than that of lead. According to the *Clinical Toxicology of Commercial Products*, 5th edition, 1984, lead is given a toxicity rating of 3 to 4, and fluoride is rated at 4 (3 = moderately toxic, 4 = very toxic).

On December 7, 1992, the new EPA Maximum Contaminant Level (MCL) for lead was set at 0.015 ppm (parts per million). The MCL for fluoride is currently set for 4.0 ppm - that's over 250 times the permissible level of lead.

The acceptable limit for fluoride was 1.0 ppm until the EPA discovered that natural fluoride levels in many towns were much higher than this and they then raised the acceptable level fourfold to 4.0 ppm.

Current fluoride intake is estimated to be between 5 and 7 mg per day in fluoridated areas. Intake is equally divided between drinking water (in fluoridated areas), food, other beverages, and dental products, meaning that even if you don't live in a fluoridated area, you are still consuming fluoride.

Average fluoride intake from juices is 0.02 to 2.80 ppm, grape juice has been found to contain up to 6.8

mg per liter, and a can of chicken soup up to 4 mg per liter.

Fluoride can be found in water, toothpaste, mouthwash, dentists' treatment, fluoride pills, juice, soft drinks, canned food, commercial fruit and vegetables, Teflon coated items, etc.

The current content of sodium fluoride in toothpaste in Canada and the US is up to 0.4%, which works out to 4000 ppm. It is known that half a tube of toothpaste can kill a child, and you do not know how much of the toothpaste that your child is using is being swallowed.

## Dental Treatment

Going to the dentist to have your teeth cleaned and fluoride treatment applied can be even more dangerous. Fluoride treatments can contain between 10,000 to 20,000 ppm of fluoride. In fact, there are known cases of children dying in the dentist's chair. (New York Times, Jan 20, 1979: "$750,000 Given in Child's Death in Fluoride Case", about a young child killed by fluoride treatment in the Dentist's office.)

Since 1997 all toothpaste in the US has to carry a warning label advising parents of what to do in case their child swallows any toothpaste over a certain amount. The warning labels on toothpaste in Canada came into effect later.

As little as 0.04 mg/day has been proven to cause adverse health effects. As little as 2 mg/day will produce crippling skeletal fluorosis in a person's lifetime. What makes this toxic compound even more insidious is that it is a cumulative substance that builds up in your body. It is estimated that only about 50% of daily fluoride intake is eliminated and the other 50% gets absorbed in calcified tissues like bone and teeth.

**Fluorosis**

Fluoride is a seriously toxic product and is the most bone-seeking element known to man. The US Public Health Service has stated that fluoride makes the bones more brittle and the dental enamel more porous. The use of fluoride on your teeth leads to something called dental fluorosis, and it is estimated that one in five children are affected by this condition.

Realistic figures of dental fluorosis are as high as 80% in some areas in the US, and as high as 69% in some areas in Canada. Studies have been conducted that directly link bone tissue damage with dental fluorosis.

Fluorosis is the first visible sign that destructive effects from the use of fluoride are taking place, and so we should look at what fluorosis is. Dental fluorosis, also called mottled teeth or mottled enamel, is a disease of the teeth that first shows up as discoloration on tooth enamel.

Healthy teeth are opaque, and are a slight off-white in color. The surface of mottled teeth generally appears to be darker than healthy teeth, with lines, flecks, or opaque white surfaces present. In moderate to severe conditions, the enamel shows severe stains, pitting, and enamel breaking off from the tooth. Fluorosis also makes teeth vulnerable to chipping and cracking.

Fluorosis is permanent damage to the enamel, which shows up as white or brown spots appearing on your teeth. When fluoride reaches the cells of the tooth, which make enamel, the cells become poisoned. As they degenerate, they lay down irregular enamel. Instead of producing regular enamel, the cells will produce mottled, porous, and thin enamel. If a lot of poison accumulates, the enamel may even be absent.

According to the US Public Health Service, fluoride makes dental enamel more porous, makes bones more brittle, and can lead to crippling arthritic deformities of the spine and major joints of the body.

We are continually bombarded with the message that fluoride is good for our teeth and that it is effective in reducing tooth decay, however, there has not been so much as one study performed that would confirm this.

The practice of putting fluoride into our drinking water is nothing less than supplying mass medication to people who are not even aware of it, and who have been medicated without their consent. We have had this toxic compound placed into our water supply without any studies supporting the concept that fluoride builds strong bones and teeth.

Our water supply is not the only place where fluoride is found, although the majority of fluoride stems from this source.

**Our Environment**

Fluoride is also known to have a serious effect on the environment. Studies have shown the adverse effects of fluoride on the ecosystem. In 1995, the CEPA identified the now closed Brunswick Mining and Smelting Fertilizer Plant in Belledune, New Brunswick, Canada, as having the largest discharge of fluoride to the aquatic environment in Canada. Toxicity to marine bacteria and impaired reproduction effects were noted.

Agriculture Canada found that twenty-five out of thirty-six cattle on several local farms displayed real or potential symptoms of chronic fluorosis. A study of livestock in the region indicated stiffness and inflamed leg joints, dental fluorosis, osteosclerosis, osteonecrosis, and bone deformations. Many serious toxic and detrimental effects to plants and animal species were documented, and salmon populations in the region were placed on the high-risk category.

There are other health problems associated with fluoride. **In 1990 the National Cancer Institute found that fluoride was a carcinogen**. In 1992 further studies revealed a 6.9% increase in bone cancer linked to fluoridated water, and as of 1997 there were over eighty references available, linking the use of fluoride to cancer.

Fluoride has repeatedly been found to be cancer causing in cell structures, in animals and in humans. Other studies reveal an increase in hip fractures, brain damage, osteoporosis, arthritis… and the list goes on.

**The FDA**

The Food and Drug Administration (FDA) considers fluoride an unapproved new drug for which there is no proof of safety or effectiveness. There are no reliable studies, conducted under ethical research guidelines, that indicate any benefits of fluoride supplementation. There are, however, more than 500 studies that indicate adverse health effects.

Also, the International Academy of Oral Medicine and Toxicology has classified fluoride as an unapproved dental medicament due to its high toxicity. The American Academy of Pediatric Dentistry has no proof of fluoride safety or effectiveness, and such proof has been required by law since June 7, 1938.

When the FDA was asked for their records of test results to verify the safety of fluoride, they initially refused to comply. They were finally pressured into admitting that they could not comply with the request because there is no drug application on record for fluoride, and none was ever submitted.

There are enormous health care costs associated with injury from fluoridation. In California alone the health effects are estimated to cost $900 million a year. Adverse health effects include hip fractures, joint and ligament calcification, bone cancers, other cancers, allergies, accidental poisoning and deaths. The cost of a hip replacement alone is around $35,000.

**Protect Yourself**

There are better ways of disposing of fluoride than by poisoning our population, and there are much better ways today of preventing tooth decay, as if that ever was the intent.

You can protect yourself from fluoride in the following manner. If you live in an area with fluoridated water, drink distilled water. There are many sources that supply this. You can also obtain reverse osmosis systems for use in the home that take fluoride out of the water.

Eliminate any Teflon coated cookware because scratches in the surface will release toxic fluoride compounds. Avoid fruit juices, canned goods, etc. that comes from fluoridated areas, especially non-organic grape products, which are especially high in fluoride because of the number of fertilizer and pesticide applications.

Contact your elected official and demand that the use of fluoride cease immediately. Do what you can to educate people in your community about the dangers of fluoride not only in water, but dental products, foods, and juices. If you live in an area where fluoridation is practiced, work with local groups to stop fluoride from being poured into your water supply.

Besides containing fluoride, there are other substances in toothpaste that you should be aware of. Toothpaste contains an abrasive to help clean your teeth, and sugar to improve the taste. The abrasive can damage your enamel and the sugar will promote tooth decay.

There are very effective alternative substances available that you can use to clean your teeth that will not damage your enamel or promote decay.

Anyone having access to the Internet may want to conduct a search using the following two key words, "amalgam" and "fluoride".

## Chapter Six

# Modern Medicine

Centuries ago, the only medicines available to man came from the herbs that grew in the ground. The people of that day taught themselves what parts of which plant to use for which ailment. The leaves of the Aloe Vera plant would likely have been used to heal burns and wounds. The bark of the birch tree may have been used for joint pain. Cascara Sagrada may have been used as a laxative, much the same as it is today.

Because of his knowledge of herbs and other healing practices, the "Medicine Man" of that day was an important and respected member of his community. His healing knowledge was passed on to selected members of each future generation for thousands of years.

Our present day pharmaceutical industry was developed from first using herbs to heal, and then we gradually introduced chemicals into our medical system. Our present day medical system has only been in existence for approximately seventy-five years, and over this period of time herbal remedies have pretty much gone by the wayside, and chemical drugs have become the medicine of choice.

## Lethal Side-effects

It is becoming increasingly evident that the use of these chemicals to treat diseases in the human body has not been a good idea. In fact, many of the chemical drugs that were used thirty years ago cannot be used today because they have been discovered to be toxic. Studies have shown that the toxic effects of these drugs are the cause of birth defects, serious long-term illness, and death.

We now know that the use of these "modern drugs" can have a negative effect on our health, and yet our pharmaceutical companies brew up more and more of these concoctions every day.

The drugs that are manufactured may perform the functions for which they are intended, but the chemicals in these drugs and their side effects are causing a lot of harm. One of the problems is that most of the drugs being manufactured are only tested for a very short period of time before they are released to the public.

Another problem, from the patient's point of view, is that they are not being told of potential side effects until these side effects occur.

Of course, if you knew of the side effects you may not be willing to take the drug. An example of this would be giving someone Prozac for chronic depression. The side effects of Prozac are dizziness, dry mouth, nausea, headache, diarrhea, insomnia, nervousness, anxiety, and increased sweating. If a patient suffering from chronic depression was facing all those side effects, he may determine that he really doesn't need Prozac after all.

Even something as common as an aspirin has serious side effects. Aspirin is suspected of causing ulcers and of damaging your kidneys with continued use, but a lot of doctors still prescribe it as a blood thinner for people who have problems with clogged arteries. Just as a point of interest, the Hazardous Chemicals Desk Reference lists the contents of aspirin as "moderately toxic by ingestion".

There are a number of drugs available for people suffering from heart disease, and all of them have serious side effects. Thrombolytic agents dissolve clots, but they give us double vision, headache, muscle pain, nausea, and shortness of breath.

Anticoagulants prevent further clotting but they give us stomach pain, blurred vision, and diarrhea. The people who put these chemicals together don't really understand what side effects we might suffer.

The side effects mentioned so far have been mild. There are other drugs being prescribed with side effects that are a lot more severe. As an example, I have included an excerpt from an article I came across in a National Magazine entitled "Death from Side-effects", which reads as follows:

*A disturbing new study by University of Toronto researchers suggests that correctly administered drugs kill an average of 106,000 people a year in the United States. That would make adverse drug reactions, or ADRs, the fourth leading cause of death.*

*The controversial report, published in the Journal of the American Medical Association (JAMA), says about 2.2 million Americans annually suffer a drug reaction severe enough to require hospitalization, prolong a hospital stay, cause death or a permanent disability.*

I was very surprised to read that correctly administered drugs kill over 100,000 people a year in the USA, but I guess I should not be.

For much more information about ADRs, you might wish to do a Google search using "Death from Side-effects".

E.R. (Ron) Harder

**Pharmaceutical Industry**

Our entire drug based pharmaceutical industry has been built on an erroneous concept. When we have a disease in our body, toxins in one form or another have built up within us. We get an indication of this through pain, swelling, or general discomfort.

We go to our doctor and he prescribes some medication for us. The medication being prescribed has very likely been manufactured using some form of chemical, and is therefore toxic to us.

What we now have is a toxic compound being put into our body to attack other toxins that have caused us to become ill in the first place. We now have two toxic elements in our body that our immune system is trying to fight off.

The prescription we have just taken will probably have some sort of side effect like a skin rash, or maybe it causes headaches. The skin rash and headache are symptoms of something else that has just gone wrong in our body. We then take another medication to cover up those symptoms, and this process goes on until our kidneys become overloaded and we end up in the hospital.

Two things have occurred here. First of all, we are putting one toxic compound into our body to fight another toxic compound that is causing a problem within us, and we are overloading our body's defense mechanism. Why would anybody do that?

Second, the headache that we now have is an indication that something else has just gone wrong within us. The medication that we are taking is designed to take our headache away, but it does not address the cause of the headache.

In other words, the medication is suppressing the SYMPTOM of a problem, but the CAUSE of the problem is still there. The medication you were given for your headache has desensitized the nerves to make it appear that the pain is gone. The pain is still there, only now you don't feel it because your nerves are numb.

When you keep taking painkillers until your headache goes away, all you are doing is covering up something in your body that has gone wrong. You still have a problem, only now you don't know it.

What I am referring to when I say that our drug based pharmaceutical industry has been built on an erroneous concept is this. The "modern medicine" we take is based on the theory of this being a particle universe. Particle theory as it relates to medicine says that we can take a certain chemical substance, place it into our body, and have this substance correct a problem that we may have.

There is no thought given as to whether or not our body will accept this substance, or if it will be rejected. We are placing a foreign substance into our body and trying to force our body to do something that it may not want to do.

This concept is basically, morally, ethically, and medically wrong. It simply goes against all aspects of nature. It absolutely has to be much easier, much more effective, and much more in line with nature's intentions, to provide our body with the materials and with the method of treatment that will allow our body to heal itself. You simply cannot inject chemical toxins into your body and expect that you will get well.

There are millions of people walking around who are on medications, but don't need to be. The medications they are taking are robbing them of their health, and of their ability to lead normal, happy, and productive lives.

An example of this is all the people who are addicted to prescription drugs. How many people do you know who are hooked on morphine or some other insidious compound that is slowly draining the life out of that person. To address that problem we now have clinics that specialize in treating prescription drug dependency.

**Liability Form**

The next time you go and see your doctor and he wants to load you up with pills and send you on your way, ask him to sign a form that says he is responsible for giving you these drugs, if he does not fully explain all the side effects, and what these side effects are likely to cause.

At the very least, you would then have the information you need so that you can make an informed decision as to whether you want to take the drug or not. That form could be filled out something like this:

*I, _____ (name of doctor) do hereby agree to the terms and conditions as set out herein. These terms and conditions are as follows: In the event that I prescribe any medications whatsoever to _____ (name of patient), I will;*

1. *Fully describe, in writing, any and all results of these medications and will inform _____ (name of patient or guardian) of any and all side effects likely to occur from this medication.*

2. *In the event these medications cause any damage, as determined by an outside medical authority, and damages not fully disclosed in article one, to the above named patient, I fully agree to compensate*

*the above named patient for any and all such damages, to the point of liquidating my personal assets, including but not limited to, stocks and bonds, real estate holdings, automobiles, marine equipment, and offshore holdings.*

*These assets shall be liquidated, without any legal proceedings, and the proceeds thereof shall be used exclusively for the purpose of reimbursing the above named patient for his/her damages.*

*This agreement is entered into this _____ day of _____, _____, in the city of _____, in the province/state of _____.*

_____ *(signature of medical professional)*

_____ *(signature of patient)*

An agreement such as this would go a long way in stopping the incredible harm being done to people every day.

It no longer surprises me that over 100,000 people a year are dying from prescription drug related problems, and that another two million are suffering severe consequences.

**Herbal Remedies**

There is an alternative to our chemical based "modern medicine" and it comes in the form of herbal remedies. These are the same herbs that our ancestors used to take care of their aches and pains, only now we know a lot more about what these herbs were designed to do, and they are proving to be very effective in the treatment of most diseases. Also, properly formulated herbal remedies do not have lethal side effects.

When I say designed, I am not talking about being designed by man, I am talking about being designed by Mother Nature, or more accurately, by our Creator. Our food products were designed to be compatible with the matrix of the human body, and our herbs were designed to be compatible with our bodies as well.

Being compatible means that our herbs were designed as food to help our body heal. Herbs, however, are a special kind of food, over and above that which we need for nourishment. Herbs were designed so that we would have some method by which we could treat the diseases that we develop within us.

We will be discussing herbs in more detail in a later chapter. All we are attempting to do here is to inform you of the pitfalls of "modern medicine" and let you

E.R. (Ron) Harder

know that your interests in medicine are probably not the same as the interests of the pharmaceutical industry.

# Chapter Seven

# Our Health Care System

The health care systems in the United States and Canada are reported to be among the finest in the world. We have highly educated doctors, professional caring nurses, very competent support staff, and in general the finest equipment money can buy.

So, why do we still have so many sick people, and so much disease? There are at least a few reasons for this, and I would like to touch on some of them here.

**Toxic Substances**

According to those in the natural health field, one reason we have so many sick people is because our system of medicine is based on toxic substances. We already have a high accumulation of toxic substances in our body because of the foods that we eat, but now we also have to contend with these substances in our medicines.

We know that toxic chemicals are the basis for our medications. And we know that toxic chemicals kill.

We know this by looking at the statistics of 100,000 people dying every year. Herbs were around long before chemicals, and now that we are learning more about their benefits and how to properly use them, herbs are quickly making a comeback.

This makes the pharmaceutical industry very nervous. They do not like anyone tampering with their profit margins, or with the power that they enjoy in the health field. They are using this power, and their money, to keep herbs from being officially recognized as an alternate form of treatment.

Toxic chemicals, with all their side effects, are officially recognized as medication. But herbs, which do not have side effects when used properly, and come straight from nature, are not. Where is the logic behind this? Our pharmaceutical industry seems to be more concerned about money, power, and control than they are about healing people.

**Preventable Surgery**

Another problem with our health care system is that surgery is sometimes performed when it is not necessary. An example of this would be removing someone's appendix. For years, nobody knew what this tiny little organ was for. The function of the appendix is to store poisons that have accumulated in the intestines until such time as the body is able to remove them.

The appendix eventually accumulates so much poison that it swells and causes you a great deal of pain. If it bursts, the poisons will go to all parts of your body, and cause you some serious problems. To avoid this life-threatening situation, the appendix is simply removed.

What should have been done is to address the situation of the toxins building up in your intestines in the first place. Clean your intestines, help your body to remove all of these toxins, and the problem with the painful appendix will take care of itself.

## Professional Abilities

Every professional's abilities are a direct reflection of the quality and the scope of the training they have received. I would like to offer my own situation as an example of this. I am unfortunate enough to have a damaged spinal column. I was occasionally required to spend an extended period of time lying on a firm surface to allow my back to heal.

During my most recent session of severe pain, I managed to have x-rays taken of my lumbar region and discovered that two disks in my lower back were compressed to the point of only being about 25% of their normal thickness.

My doctor's prognosis was that I just had to live with it, there was nothing that could be done. Damaged disks do not grow back.

That turns out not to be true. I located a master herbalist who introduced me to one product that has removed the inflammation of the disks, and he provided me with another product that restored the damaged disks. My doctor in this case had never received any training in herbal medicine, and therefore had no idea of what herbs can do.

I mention this to let you know that your doctor is not all-knowing. Doctors are only as good as the training they have received, and the experience they have managed to accumulate, no different than any other profession.

This is not meant to suggest that doctors are not required. When a disease has been allowed to progress past the point of medical treatment being effective, and surgery becomes necessary, a doctor is certainly required. This also applies to life threatening situations such as accidents, broken bones, etc.

Between improper motivation, addressing the symptom instead of the cause, and using toxic substances to "cure" disease, you now have a good idea why we are in such a mess with our health care system.

I can also understand why it would be very difficult to initiate any change, but I do have one suggestion. Initiate a policy whereby your doctor does not get paid until he has found the CAUSE of your problem, and has cured you.

Don't you think that would clean up our health care system in one awful hurry? That takes care of motivation, the symptom instead of the cause problem, and the use of toxic substances all at the same time.

## Corrective Medicine

What we have in our society is a system where most of the emphasis is placed on corrective medicine and very little emphasis, if any, is placed on preventive medicine. We only address a health issue after we become ill. We wait until our heart is in trouble and our lungs are filling with fluid before we start to pay attention to our health. When we are young, we are immortal, and when our body finally gives out we expect to find a solution in a pill.

My ancestors had an adage that went something like this; *"An ounce of prevention is worth a pound of cure."* I used to think that this was just a bunch of old people talking, but I now realize how absolutely 100% right they were.

Along that same line, it has been estimated that the cost of preventive medicine is only about 10% of the cost of corrective medicine. This means that if we do not spend one dollar today to take care of our health, we will spend ten dollars tomorrow to try to get our health back. This does not take into account all the pain and suffering we will endure.

## Cruel Deception

We mentioned earlier that the medical establishment is motivated by money, and the ultimate example of being motivated by money and not by the desire to find a cure, is the cruel deception that we all know of called, "Searching For The Cure For Cancer".

It seems like "The Search for a Cure" has been going on for a thousand years. Entire careers have been built on it. Huge organizations have been built that serve no other function than to "Find A Cure". Large corporations, whose only purpose is to raise research funds, have grown up because of "The Search For A Cure".

I call it a cruel deception because I have seen the faces of people who are dying of cancer giving their life savings to an organization involved in cancer research. These people honestly believe that by giving their money to research, someone else may not have to suffer from this disease.

Little do they know that they are giving their money to an organization that has every intention of keeping this deception alive. Little do they know that the people who run the cancer industry will never announce a cure for cancer, business is just too good.

Billions upon billions of dollars have reportedly been spent on "research" and the only half-way effective thing our brilliant minds have come up with is "chemotherapy". In most cases, the chemotherapy does a lot of damage to your body. Also, even if the chemotherapy kills the cancer and the patient survives, the cancer frequently returns.

To give you an idea of how lucrative the cancer business really is, I would like to quote portions of an article I came across in the September 3, 2012 edition of *Newsweek* magazine. The article is entitled "How Much Would You Pay For Three More Months Of Life?"

It talks about new cancer drugs that have come on the market in the last few years, and the tremendously high prices that we have to pay for these drugs.

For example, a new wonder drug called Perjeta, when combined with Herceptin, can delay advanced breast cancer's growth for about six months, but at a cost of $188,000.

Another drug called Provenge, which is used for prostate cancer, can give a patient an average of four more months, but at a cost of about $93,000. I was absolutely floored when I read these numbers.

This article goes on for two pages and talks about the rising cost of health care, patients paying $120,000 for four injections of something called Yervoy, how much would someone be willing to pay to extend their life for six months, etc.

The bottom line is this. The pharmaceutical companies have joined forces and have a monopoly on prescription drugs. When asked why these drugs cost so much, it was simply stated that they have to recover the cost of research and development. Of course they do.

If you have no competition, and you tell people you are trying to save their lives, you can charge whatever you want for the drugs. Why are prices so high? Prices are high because they can be.

Patients have no other source for these new "wonder drugs". In my opinion, this is all about greed and corruption in the cancer industry.

Do these drugs cure cancer? NO. Will the pharmaceutical companies ever come up with a cure for cancer? NO. As mentioned previously, business is just too good.

For your information, Americans spent $23 billion for cancer drugs in 2011, and that number keeps going up.

## Some Thoughts On Healing

I have witnessed family members, friends, and strangers pass away from cancer, and in my opinion, most of these deaths could have been prevented, simply by providing the body with the "tools" that it needs to help it to defeat this disease. What are these tools? They are quality nutrition, healing herbs, enzymes, and probiotics. Above that, it is also extremely important to keep your body clean internally. We will talk about all of these later in this book.

The conventional medical establishment is all about money, and they use this money to influence our politicians to keep healing herbs and alternative medicine from being recognized as an official form of treatment.

## The Choice Is Yours

We are all responsible for our own health. Each of us has to take control of what we put into our body, and how we treat it. Health does not come in the form of a pill. Health only comes from a proper diet, removing toxins from your body, keeping your body clean internally, and from mild exercise.

A proper diet consists of food that is compatible with the electrical matrix of our body, keeping your body clean means removing the toxins that we build up within us, and mild exercise means cardiovascular exercise, which will strengthen your heart and give you a chance to live a life that is disease free. We will cover all of these in the following chapters.

## Chapter Eight

# The Cost of Health Care

As we all know, the health care costs in North America are out of control. The various levels of government are hard pressed to keep up with the increasing demands for services, and our hospitals are full. We have shortages everywhere. Most hospitals cannot find enough nurses to take care of an increasing number of patients.

Many doctors are working up to sixty hours a week. The cost of a hospital stay keeps going up, and if you are fortunate enough to survive your operation, you are released almost immediately to make room for someone else.

How did we get into this mess? We have the finest facilities money can buy and we have the highest educated medical professionals in the world. Our health care system is in chaos, and the demands of our health care system are putting a tremendous strain on our ability to pay for it all, and there really is no end in sight.

There are at least a few reasons for the tremendous cost of our health care, and I would like to touch on some of them here.

In Canada, all we have to do is go to our doctor, tell him our problems, and he will give us a pill to make the pain go away. In most cases this will not cost us one dollar. There are some obvious things wrong with this.

First of all, there is a tendency for some people to take advantage of our medical system in that they go to their doctor for almost everything. They seem to have aches and pains everywhere, and they abuse the medical system. Going to the doctor seems to be pretty much a social activity.

We absolutely have to realize that running to the clinic with every little thing that ails us costs a huge amount of money. We may not think we pay for it, but yes, we do. It comes out of our tax dollars and is part of our government's fiscal budget.

Second, our doctor is, in most cases, treating the symptom of something that has gone wrong in our body instead of addressing the cause of the problem. Making the pain go away is only temporary relief for something that may develop into a very serious condition.

Third, statistics show that the diagnosis for a medical condition is only correct about 20% of the time. This means that we will likely go back for the same problem four more times before our doctor figures out what is wrong.

What all this tells me is that we rely far too much on our health care provider to take care of us, and we do not take the time to take care of ourselves.

The time has come for us to take more responsibility for our own well-being. Most of us know when we have something seriously wrong. Having a small headache or maybe a sore muscle can usually be traced to something we are doing or have done. In that case, we should stop what we are doing and give our body time to recuperate. These are minor discomforts and not something to see your doctor about.

Health care is a business. Every time you go to your doctor, either you or your health plan has to pay a certain amount for the visit. Your doctor really doesn't care if you needed his services or not. He is very likely quite happy to write out a prescription for you and send you on your way, because he gets paid by the health plan for the visit, and by the pharmaceutical company for "selling" you the pills.

What we have discussed so far only covers a portion of your health care costs. Another huge expense is the cost of all the operations being performed every year that could have been prevented. A statistic I saw the other day stated that approximately 300,000 heart bypass operation are performed in the US every year.

I do not have accurate numbers on the average cost of a heart operation, but with everything included it is probably around $20,000 per operation. If my estimate for the average operation is correct, the money spent or lost, just because of heart bypass surgery, would be somewhere around six billion ($6,000,000,000) dollars a year. I certainly do not begrudge anyone a needed operation, but most of these operations could be avoided simply by taking better care of ourselves.

**Health Statistics**

I came across a few statistics that will give you an idea of how serious an issue health care really is. These statistics were from 2012 and they came from the American Cancer Society.

*About 1,638,910 new cancer cases were expected to be diagnosed in 2012. This estimate did not include carcinoma in situ (non-invasive cancer) of any site except urinary bladder, and did not include basal and squamous cell skin cancers, which are not required to be reported to cancer registries.*
*In 2012, about 577,190 Americans were expected to die of cancer, more than 1,500 people a day. Cancer is the second most common cause of death in the US,*

*exceeded only by heart disease, accounting for nearly 1 of every 4 deaths.*

*\*Scientific evidence suggests that up to one-third of the 577,190 cancer deaths expected to have occurred were related to nutrition, and could have been prevented.*

I find it shocking that the American Cancer Society is telling us that one third of cancer deaths are related to diet, and yet very little is being done to educate the general public about the toxins and contaminants that cause us to develop this disease. These statements by the American Cancer Society tell us what the facts are, and yet most of us just seem to ignore them.

What this tells me is that the people in a position to do something about all of this either do not care, or it is not in their best interest to take action. This once again tells me that cancer research is very much a business, it is not about finding a cure.

We have discussed the cost of our health in monetary terms, but there is another cost involved, and that is the cost of human suffering. If you really want to see human suffering, and you want to see the effects of disease, go down to your local hospital and walk through one of the wards.

Take a good look at the people suffering from cancer and heart disease, and imagine yourself in their place.

The truth is, you will be in their place if you do not take control of your own health. That person lying in that bed and fighting for each and every breath could be you.

## *Chapter Nine*

# **Your PH Level**

The PH level of your body has serious implications when it comes to the level of your health. We have known about PH for a number of years, but we have not been aware of the importance of PH where our health is concerned.

Let's take a look at what PH is.

PH is an acronym for "Potential of Hydrogen", and is a value that indicates the acidity or alkalinity of a liquid. Every liquid has a PH value, which falls on a scale between 0 and 14, with 7 being neutral. A PH value less than 7 is acidic, values greater than 7 indicate alkalinity.

The human body also has a PH value. In fact, each of your body fluids has its own level of PH, but your blood and your saliva most accurately reflect the acidity or alkalinity of your entire body.

A number of studies have been completed that tell us the following: Disease cannot flourish within us if our body is in an alkaline condition, it can only flourish within us if our body is in an acidic condition.

What does this mean? It means that it is the PH level of our body that determines the state of our health. Kindly allow me to explain.

All of the foods that we eat, and all of the liquids that we drink have their own PH level, and the PH level of the things that we consume will determine the PH level of our body. If we consistently consume foods that are acidic, we cannot help but have an acidic condition within us.

So how do I get my body into an alkaline condition? There are a number of things that you should not do, and a number of things that you should do, and I would like to mention some of them here.

It seems that a lot of us are emotionally attached to our frying pans, and we fry everything that we can get our hands on. What we do not know is that the intense heat of frying our food breaks down the oils and fats in our food, or the frying oils, and makes them very acidic. This heat creates a PH level in our food somewhere in the range of 3 to 5, depending on the type of oils or fats being used.

Also, a lot of us have an addiction to soda pop. You know, all those drinks you see advertised on billboards that "refresh" you. Most of these soft drinks have a PH between 3 and 4, and should not be consumed. They produce a very high acidic condition in your body, and cause you all kinds of serious health problems.

The two items mentioned above are a big reason for the acidic conditions in our body, but another reason is the type of food that we consume.

As mentioned above, our foods all have their own PH level, and so the foods that we consume have a huge impact on the PH level of our body.

Your body works hard to maintain a balanced PH because that allows its systems to operate more efficiently and effectively. Imbalance, on the other hand, leads to obesity, fatigue, premature aging, and serious health problems.

To try to maintain a balanced PH, your body pulls certain minerals, like sodium, potassium, calcium and magnesium from its tissues to neutralize acids in the blood. If it can't do that successfully, it will dump the acids into various organs, which will cause serious health concerns. This is discussed in more detail in the section below.

You can help your body neutralize acids and maintain a balanced PH by being selective about the kinds of food that you consume.

The following is a list of foods that indicate Acid, Neutral or Alkaline. It is included here to give you an idea of the acidity/alkalinity level of the various types of foods.

## ACIDIC FOODS:

All fried foods - Alcohol - Artificial Sweeteners - Asparagus - Beef - Beer - Brussel Sprouts - Butter - Carob - Catsup - Cheese - Chicken - Cocoa - Chocolate - Coffee - Corn - Corn Starch - Cranberries - Flour - Jam - Jelly - Ice Cream - Lard - Lobster - Mussels - Nuts - Oat Bran - Oils - Peas - Pork - Rye - Soybeans - Soy Milk - Sugar - Tomatoes - Veal.

## NEUTRAL FOODS:

Apples - Bananas - Beans - Blueberries - Brazil Nuts - Buckwheat - Cauliflower - Carrots - Cherries - Chestnuts - Dates - Eggplant - Eggs - Figs - Fish - Goat Cheese - Grapes - Honey - Lemons - Lettuce - Lima Beans - Maple Syrup - Millet - Milk - Oatmeal - Organic Olive Oil - Flaxseed Oil - Oranges - Peaches - Pears - Pineapple - Plums - Pumpkin - Raisons - Brown Rice - Strawberries - Turkey.

## ALKALINE FOODS:

Almonds - Baking Soda - Blackberries - Broccoli - Cantaloupe - Cinnamon - Coconut - Daikon Radish - Garlic - Grapefruit - Honeydew - Kale - Lentils -

Limes - Mangos - Molasses - Mustard Greens - Nectarines - Onions - Papayas - Peppers - Poppy Seeds - Raspberries - Sea Salt - Sea Vegetables - Soy Sauce - Sweet Potatoes - Tangerines - Watermelon - Yams.

There appears to be a discrepancy between various alkaline/acidic food lists, and that is because some foods that are alkaline or acidic may change slightly once they are absorbed by your body.

For a more comprehensive list of alkaline/acidic foods, and much more information, you may wish to visit the following web site.

https://liveenergized.com/wp-content/uploads/ 2013/02/acid-alkaline-food-chart- 2.0.pdf

The above web site contains the most comprehensive acid/alkaline web site that I have come across, and I hope you find the information on that website helpful.

There are two more items that I would like to mention about the PH level in your body.

First, a low PH level in your blood also means a low level of oxygen, and a low level of oxygen in your blood means that you are much more likely to develop cancer, or any other disease.

Second, 7.0 is the neutral point of PH in your body. Anything above that is considered alkaline, anything below that is considered acidic. Now, if you have a PH of 5.0, it is not two times more acidic as 7.0, it is twenty times more acidic.

The PH numbers multiply by a factor of ten when they refer to various levels. A PH level of 4.0 will make that liquid thirty times more acidic than something that has a PH level of 7.0. Something having a PH of 4.0 is not slightly more acidic, it is a lot more acidic.

To give you an idea of how serious an issue this is, I had occasion to attend a demo on alkaline water recently, and here was this can of pop with a PH of 3.5, and next to it was this large container of alkaline water with a PH of 9.0.

The objective was to neutralize the acid in that can of pop, and it took the equivalent of twelve cans of alkaline water to accomplish that. So, if you drink one can of soda pop, it will take the equivalent of twelve cans of alkaline water with a PH of 9.0 to bring your body back to a neutral state. Think of the negative effect that can of pop will have on your body.

Please Note: The PH level of your body is the single most important item that will determine the overall state of your health, now and into the near future. So how can you find out what your PH level is? There is a very easy method that you can use at home to accomplish that.

Go down to your drug store, or your local health food store, and pick up something called Litmus Paper. This is a paper compound that will change color when it comes into contact with an acidic or alkaline liquid. It also comes with a color chart that will let you know the PH level of any liquid.

To use this method, place a few drops of saliva on the Litmus Paper and take note of the change in its color. Refer to the color chart included to determine the PH level of your saliva. Very simple and easy to use.

## Chapter Ten

# Water

When someone mentions water, we visualize something so abundant in our world that we hardly give it a second thought. In most places in North America we just turn on the tap and there it is. We do not appreciate how vital a commodity water is, and we may not realize that without water there would be no life on this earth.

What is water? Water is a clear, colorless, odorless liquid that is formed by combining two elements of hydrogen with one element of oxygen to form water vapor ($H_2O$), and then combining three $H_2O$ molecules to form liquid water.

### Water In Our Body

When we think of water in terms of our health we have to consider how water is used in our bodies. In addition to offering true refreshment for our thirst, water plays a significant role in all bodily processes, including digestion, absorption of nutrients, muscle contraction, circulation, lubrication of body joints, and removing toxins from the body,

Water is the transporter of all nutrients throughout our body, and it is essential for all building functions. Water helps maintain normal body temperature through perspiration, and it is responsible for the removal of waste products.

It is also the key ingredient for maximum athletic performance, and makes the difference between feeling energized or feeling exhausted after a workout.

Oxygen is ranked as the number one substance essential for life, and water is ranked as number two. We can live for some period of time without shelter or clothing, we can live for a shorter period of time without food, we can live for several days without water, but we do not live at all without oxygen.

Water makes up somewhere from 60% to 70% of the total body weight in humans. Males normally have a higher percentage of body water than females, and this is because females very often have more body fat. Fat tissue is composed of oils, not water. The following chart is a breakdown of what specific body parts contain how much water.

| Teeth & Bones | 10% | Lungs | 80% |
|---|---|---|---|
| Cartilage | 55% | Brain | 80% |
| Liver | 70% | Blood | 90% |
| Muscles | 75% | Lymph | 90% |
| Spleen | 75% | Saliva | 95% |

Most fruit that you eat and most juices that you drink have a high water content. Meat products contain up to 70% water, and vegetables contain up to 95%. Even foods that you may think of as being dry, such as some cereals, can contain up to 25% water.

Adults should drink up to 4 glasses of water a day to maintain healthy bodily functions. It has been said that a lot of this water is supplied by the food that you eat, but that is not true.

Water is required for all of your body functions, and if you do not make enough water available to perform those functions you will be in a state of dehydration. Symptoms of dehydration can be headaches, small aches and pains in your joints and muscles, low energy levels, stomach discomforts, and just a general feeling of not being up to par. Before you run off to your doctor, try drinking a glass or two of water, and most of these symptoms will likely disappear.

A lot of the water in our body is lost through nothing more than breathing. You can see the moisture that you expel if you breathe directly onto your reading glasses. It is estimated that we lose about 8 ounces of water through breathing over the course of one night.

This then says that we can become dehydrated while we sleep. If you wake up in the morning feeling tired and you really don't want to get out of bed, you may be dehydrated, and the first thing you should do is drink one glass of water. This will replenish the water that you have lost overnight through breathing.

Some people believe that you should not drink water with, or immediately after, a meal. The reasoning behind this is that drinking water at this time will dilute the digestive juices and enzymes in your digestive tract, and will make digestion much more difficult.

This is absolutely not true. Water is required for all activity in your body, and especially digestion. Digestion involves breaking down your food particles into a liquid form so that your body can absorb your food more easily, and this definitely requires water.

**Sources Of Drinking Water**

Most of us have our drinking water supplied to us by the local water authority, and all we have to do in our homes is open a tap. The water that is delivered to our homes is generally obtained either from a surface water supply, such as a lake or river, or from a ground water supply such as a well.

There are two types of wells, a surface well and a drilled well. A surface well is dug by an excavating machine, and it simply consists of a hole in the ground, normally about fifteen feet deep and three feet wide, where surface water collects. This type of well can carry many forms of impurities such as animal feces, and other substances that are found on the surface of the ground.

A drilled well consists of a shaft drilled through the earth to a water table below the surface, and this water is then pumped to the surface by means of a submersible pump. A drilled well is preferred over a surface well and is normally used as the public water supply source if a river or a lake is not available.

**Is Your Water Safe?**

Most people assume that when they turn on the kitchen tap they are getting clean, safe drinking water. Unfortunately, this is not the case in most of North America. Because of industrial pollution, modern farming practices, and various commercial activities, our drinking water has been degraded to the point where it now contains a number of different types of toxic substances.

The drinking water in most towns and cities is processed, which means that it is filtered to remove some unwanted substances, or it may have chemicals added to it to kill harmful bacteria. It is up to the individual to find out how their drinking water is treated, and to determine how safe the water is that comes out of their taps.

If you are concerned about the safety of your tap water, you can contact your local public health authority and ask them how to go about having your tap water tested.

One word of caution, some health departments only check for bacterial content, not toxic substances, and so you may want to have a local commercial laboratory check your tap water for its chemical content as well.

Here is some information that you might want to know. The National Resources Defense Council (NRDC) found that over 18,000 of the water supplies in the US had unacceptable levels of contaminants. These contaminants were blamed for 900,000 illnesses in a one-year period, and 100 deaths.

Contaminants in untreated water also cause problems in other parts of the world. In Peru, for example, an epidemic that spread to six other Latin American countries caused 600,000 cases of cholera and killed

E.R. (Ron) Harder

5,000 people. These deaths were a direct result of not treating their water supplies.

Besides disease, there are a number of other substances in your water supplies that have a dramatic impact on your health.

Substances such as chlorine, carbon, lime, phosphates, soda ash, and aluminum sulfate are intentionally added to your drinking water in an effort to kill bacteria, adjust the PH level, and eliminate cloudiness.

Other substances such as fertilizers, asbestos, cyanides, herbicides, pesticides, and industrial chemicals, may leach into your water supplies through the soil, or perhaps from water supply and plumbing pipes. Still other substances, such as arsenic, iron, lead, copper and other heavy metals, may also leach into your water supplies from the soil.

**Five Major Concerns**

The biggest concerns about water safety today come from contaminants such as chlorine, sodium fluoride, pesticides, parasites, and something called MTBE. These can all cause serious health problems. Let's take a look at these.

## Chlorine

The first major concern is chlorine. Chlorine has long been added to your water supply to kill harmful bacteria, and I have no doubt that it does this job well.

Chlorine was used during the First World War to kill enemy troops, and now we use it in our water supplies and in our swimming pools to kill bacteria. Chlorine kills all bacteria, including the bacteria in your digestive system that you need to digest your food.

Not only does chlorine kill all bacteria, it will also kill all the enzymes that it comes into contact with. Without enzymes, your body cannot function.

Even in a very diluted form, chlorine causes two serious conditions to occur in your body, and they are as follows:

Some by-products of chlorine are now known to be carcinogenic. One such by-product, trihalomethanes (THMs), is formed when chlorine reacts with organic materials, such as leaves or soil in water.

Also, chlorine in water, combined with animal fats in the diet, results in the production of a sticky substance that adheres to arterial walls and causes atherosclerosis. Atherosclerosis is the major cause of heart disease, as discussed in a previous chapter.

The issue of chlorine is serious enough that you would be well-advised to keep it entirely away from your body. You can purchase chlorine filters that will remove this toxic compound from your water supply.

To remove chlorine from your kitchen you can purchase filters that simply hook up to your kitchen tap. To remove chlorine from your bathroom you can purchase filters that connect to your shower-head or to your bathroom tap. To ensure your whole house is safe, you can install in-line chlorine water filters that will connect into your water line entering your home.

For your information, chlorine will be absorbed into your body eight times faster by having a shower than by drinking chlorinated water.

Also, most public swimming pools have chlorine added to the water to kill any bacteria that may be in the pool. Use your own good judgment as to whether or not you want to swim there.

**Sodium Fluoride**

The second major concern is sodium fluoride, which was discussed in a previous chapter as well. Sodium fluoride has uses other than what we previously mentioned. They include cockroach powder, fumigants, insecticides, fungicides, germicides and solvents. It is also very effective as a rat poison. As mentioned, there are medical reports that tell us that fluoride is carcinogenic. Great stuff to be putting into your drinking water.

## Pesticides

The third major concern is the presence of pesticides, and these are found in any area where the tap water comes from an underground source. Pesticides are used extensively in farming practices, and especially in orchards and vineyards to control insects that feed on fruits and vegetables.

When a field is sprayed, the pesticides drain down through the soil and leach into the aquifer below the ground. This aquifer is your underground water supply.

**Pesticides are known carcinogens**, and also cause numerous other health problems that affect all parts of your body. These chemicals are persistent, and are still found in the underground water supply decades after pesticides are no longer used for pest control.

## Parasites

The fourth major concern is parasites, and among these, a parasite called cryptosporidium is causing the most concern. Residents from several major cities were recently forced to boil their tap water after unacceptable levels of cryptosporidium were found in their water supplies, most likely coming from agricultural runoff.

These parasites suppress the immune system and therefore can be lethal to anyone who suffers from HIV or AIDS.

Cryptosporidium is commonly found in lakes and rivers and is most common in water that is contaminated with sewage and animal waste. This parasite is resistant to disinfection and cannot be killed by adding chlorine to the water. Even a well-operated water treatment system cannot guarantee that its drinking water will be free of this parasite.

**MTBE**

The fifth major concern is MTBE (methyl-t-butyl ether). MTBE is a member of a group of chemicals known as fuel oxygenates, which are added to gasoline to increase its oxygen content. It is used to reduce carbon monoxide and ozone levels caused by automobile emissions, and has been used as a lead replacement since 1979.

The health damages caused by MTBE have not yet been fully determined, but they are believed to be extensive. More than forty projects are reported to be underway to assess the risk of MTBE on your health.

## Chemical Contaminants

There are numerous other contaminants in our water supplies and they can generally be listed under three categories. These are Inorganic Chemicals, Synthetic Organic Chemicals, and Volatile Organic Chemicals.

Under Inorganic Chemicals we find substances such as Asbestos, Barium, Cadmium, Chromium, Mercury, Nitrates, Lead, Copper, Cyanide, and Thallium. I'm sure you recognize that most of these are extremely toxic.

There are approximately thirty more contaminants listed under Synthetic Organic Chemicals, and approximately twenty-five more contaminants listed under Volatile Organic Chemicals that could likely be found in your drinking water. The majority of these toxins come from industry and agriculture.

Some of the safety standards that we are quoted indicate that a certain level of lead may be safe, a certain level of asbestos may be safe, and a certain level of mercury may be safe. This is absolutely not true.

Also, what they do not tell you is that these toxins accumulate in your body faster than you can eliminate them, and as these toxins accumulate, the combined health effects on your body can be devastating.

## Minerals In Water

Some of the minerals that are essential for life, such as sodium, potassium, calcium, copper, and magnesium, can also be found in your drinking water. We use calcium for our bones and in blood clotting, and we use magnesium to produce energy and to carry out nerve impulses.

Copper is required to strengthen the walls of our veins, and sodium is required for perspiration to help our bodies cool.

The different concentrations of these minerals in your water determine whether your water is considered to be hard or soft. Hard water contains high amounts of calcium and magnesium, which is responsible for the crystal residue in your kettle. Most people prefer soft water because it dissolves soap better, and leaves very little residue behind.

There are a few ways that you can improve your tap water and filtering seems to be the most common. Try to use a filter that will remove particles of one micrometer or less in diameter. This should take out most parasites, microorganisms, and other contaminants.

For those who are concerned about cryptosporidium, boiling your water for one minute is the most effective method of killing this parasite. If boiling the water you use for drinking and cooking is not a reasonable option, you may wish to purchase bottled water.

**Bottled Water**

Bottled water is usually classified by where it originates, by the mineral content of the water, or by the type of treatment it has undergone. Some bottled water goes through more than one treatment process and can be classified under more than one category.

Some classes of bottled water are as follows:

a) De-mineralized Water. When the adding or removing of electrons has neutralized the electric charge in the water, it is said to be de-mineralized or de-ionized. This de-mineralizing takes out the nitrates and the minerals calcium and magnesium. It also removes the heavy metals cadmium, barium, lead, and some radium. These are some of the Inorganic Chemicals we discussed previously.

b) Mineral Water. This is natural spring water, and sometimes comes from Canada or from some parts of Europe. To be called mineral water it must have minerals, it must flow freely from its source, it cannot be forced from the ground through pumping action, and it must be bottled at the same location where it is obtained.

You may wish to inquire as to which minerals this water contains because the minerals will vary with the source.

If you drink water that has minerals you do not need, your body may become overloaded with these minerals and they may in fact cause you harm. Also, be aware that some manufacturers add bicarbonates, citrates, or sodium phosphates to filtered water and call it mineral water.

c)   Natural Spring Water. This is the same as Mineral Water except that it is supposed to have come from a spring. This water has not had its mineral content altered but it may have been filtered or treated, and flavoring may have been added.

d)   Sparkling Water. Sparkling water is water that has been carbonated. This normally has the same mineral content as when it left the ground, and is called sparkling because it has been carbonated from a separate source.

e)   Distilled Water. This is the purest form of water available and is one of the better types of water you should be drinking.

The water is heated, forms into water vapor, cools, and forms back into water. This process kills any bacteria or other live contaminants that may have been in the original water, and through the process of evaporation and condensation most of the other impurities are left behind.

All other sources of bottled water still contain some of the chemicals and toxins that were in the water when it was in the ground, even though the water may have been filtered or treated. Not all elements in our water supplies can be totally removed through the filtering and treatment processes.

**Alkalized Water**

Another form of water that has become popular is alkalized water. We discussed your PH level in a previous chapter, and this is what alkalized water refers to. Help your body to raise its PH level by drinking only alkalized water.

There are now a number of machines available that will increase the PH of your drinking water up to 9.0 or slightly higher. Some of these machines serve more than one purpose, they will also ionize your water so that it has a charge of minus 300 milli-volts. What this does is supply millions of free electrons to the water to help you combat free radical damage in your body, especially to the tissues of your heart.

Some of these machines connect directly to your kitchen tap. They purify this water through filtering down as low as .5 microns, they alkalize the water, and they ionize it. This process removes almost all of the impurities.

There are other systems available that will increase the PH level of your water, without ionizing it. These are simply filter systems that remove most of the more common toxins, and supplying the alkalizing agents in the filtering process.

In my opinion, alkalized and ionized water is the only water you should be drinking, because of the tremendous health benefits that this type of water can provide to your body. I would recommend a minimum of four glasses of alkalized/ionized water a day.

More information has recently come to light about the huge benefits that water can have for your body, but it is more than can be included here. If you would like to take a look at some of this information you can read an article listed on the following web site:

www.naturalscience.org/fileadmin/.../report_**water_** en.pdf

## Chapter Eleven

# The Benefits of Exercise

No book on health would be complete without at least one chapter on exercise. There are some benefits to exercise that you may not be aware of, and I would like to cover some of those benefits here.

Your body needs exercise to survive, and to maintain its physical strength. You can see proof of this in people who for one reason or another are forced to be idle. For example, if you break a bone in your arm and have to wear a cast, the muscle tissue in that arm will become weak and will decrease in size. After your cast has been removed, it will take a while to regain your muscle mass and restore the strength that you had before.

The human body is a magnificent and complex structure. It consists of some six hundred and fifty muscles that supply movement to over two hundred various bones. Each muscle consists of individual components that work together as one large unit to provide movement to the body, and all of this is controlled by your central nervous system.

The bones that make up your skeletal structure are usually thought of as solid structures, but this is not the case. Your bones are actually living, breathing, and porous structures that serve more than one purpose. Besides supporting your body, your bones are the place where your red blood cells are manufactured.

This manufacturing is done in the marrow of the bones and a lot of blood cells are produced in a very short period of time. It is estimated that within one second, approximately three million red blood cells will be produced to replace the ones that your body loses.

All parts of your body benefit from regular exercise. This is true for all muscle tissue, all organs, and the skeletal structure. Exercising brings flexibility to the joints, increases the blood supply to all parts of your body, and helps you to remove toxins and waste products.

One other important benefit of exercise is that by increasing the blood flow to all parts of your body, you are also increasing the amount of oxygen that your blood delivers to your cells.

As was stated previously, all disease conditions are accompanied by an oxygen deficiency at the cellular level, therefore, when you exercise, you increase the blood flow to your cells and you increase the amount of oxygen that gets delivered to your cells at the same time.

The delivery of more blood to your cells could very well be the single most important benefit that you receive from regular exercise. If you exercise infrequently, or not at all, you are likely one of the 80% of people who do not get sufficient amounts of oxygen to their cells to maintain a healthy body.

**Your Exercise Program**

Before starting an exercise program, talk with your health care provider and find out about the risks of exercise. Find out what form of exercise is safe for you, and would fit in with your lifestyle.

Find out if you have any major medical problems that would limit your exercise program, what these problems are, and what you can do to work around those problems. Start with any exercise program that you can, and you will be surprised at how quickly you will become healthier.

A few words of caution before you start with your exercise program.

a) Avoid strenuous exercise during the hottest part of the day. In warm climate regions this would be between 11 am and 4 pm. Exercising in hot weather will make you susceptible to heatstroke and exhaustion.

b) Avoid strenuous exercise in a cold climate. It can lead to a frozen air passage and frozen lungs, which can cause severe damage. Also, if exercising in a cold environment, dress in layers so that you can discard clothing as necessary to avoid perspiration.

c) Make certain to drink water before, during, and after exercising to avoid dehydration.

d) Wear loose fitting clothing to allow for perspiration to evaporate.

e) Take a fifteen minute break when your body requires it. This thing about "no pain - no gain" can be extremely dangerous.

f) Do not exercise beyond your abilities. Pushing yourself beyond your limits can lead to very serious problems with your heart and with your extremities.

g) Wait for one hour after a meal before you begin exercising. Your body is busy digesting food during this one hour, and energy is not readily available for other purposes.

h) Try to exercise in clean air. Jogging next to a busy freeway is not advisable because of all the exhaust fumes from passing vehicles. Exercising outdoors in or near big cities is also not advisable because of ozone, smog, carbon monoxide, sulfur dioxide etc. Try to exercise in a location where the air is fresh and clean.

## Aerobic Exercise

It is now generally recognized that of all the exercises that we do, aerobic exercise is the most beneficial. Aerobic exercise refers to a rhythmic exercise activity that uses large muscle groups, and can be maintained for an extended period of time. Examples of this would be walking, slow jogging, swimming, cycling, skiing, hiking, etc.

Walking is perhaps the most common because it can be done anywhere, and does not require special equipment beyond a good pair of shoes. Regular physical exercise will give you more stamina, it will increase your strength, and you will have less chance of injury.

The term aerobic exercise can also be called cardiovascular exercise because it has the most benefit on the cardiovascular system. Cardiovascular exercise provides many benefits that cannot be obtained by any other activity. These exercises benefit the heart, the lungs, and the arteries. They will also decrease high blood pressure, lower high cholesterol, reduce stress, and help you with any weight problems.

Cardiovascular exercise is also convenient. You can do it outdoors or indoors, while watching TV, or reading a book.

Some of the benefits of cardiovascular exercise come from its direct effect on the muscles of the heart. The amount of work the heart has to do depends upon your body's oxygen requirements and your blood pressure, and with regular exercise the heart muscles become stronger and are able to pump more blood with a lower heart rate.

Also, through regular exercise your heart muscles will increase in size, which will allow your heart to pump the same amount of blood with less effort. Exercise also stimulates the growth of the coronary arteries, which supply blood to your heart.

Some people believe that vigorous exercise will bring on a heart attack. This is true only if your heart does not receive regular exercise, your heart is weak, or you suddenly engage in a vigorous activity. If you do not have cardiovascular problems, if you exercise regularly, and if you exercise in moderation, a heart attack while exercising is very unlikely.

**Your Heart**

We should discuss the heart for a moment so we can see what a marvelous organ it is. The heart is the center of the cardiovascular system. It is about the size of a human fist and weighs only about ten ounces. The heart is made up of four chambers. There are two upper atrium chambers, and two lower ventricle chambers. (See Figure 7 in this chapter.)

The right atrium and right ventricle work together to receive blood from the veins in the body and pump it to the lungs. The left atrium and left ventricle work together to receive blood from the lungs and pump it to the rest of your body.

A portion of the blood that the left ventricle pumps to your body is routed to the heart itself, through the aorta and the coronary arteries. There are two main coronary arteries leading from the aorta to the heart, and these are the left and the right arteries.

The left coronary artery supplies the right atrium, most of the right ventricle, and part of the left ventricle. The left coronary artery supplies the left atrium, and most of the left ventricle.

Adequate blood supply to the left ventricle is essential because it is the left ventricle that delivers blood to almost all of the body, including the heart itself.

The heart actually consists of two pumps that deliver blood to the lungs, to the rest of the body, and to itself. It sits in a triple layered bag called the pericardium, which protects the heart, yet allows it freedom of movement for vigorous and rapid contractions.

At rest, the heart pumps about one gallon of blood per minute, or about 1,440 gallons of blood per day. The heart pumps blood through all of your blood vessels and works twenty-four hours a day, 365 days a year, without rest, supplying nutrients and oxygen to your cells.

**Blood Pressure**

We mentioned blood pressure before so let's take a look at what it is. Blood pressure is the pressure on the walls of the arteries as the heart pumps blood through them. The arteries are able to expand, and each time the heart contracts it forces blood through the arteries. This puts pressure on the artery walls and stretches them. The pressure when the heart pumps is called the systolic blood pressure.

When the heart is between beats the pressure on the artery walls is decreased. The walls now contract and maintain a lower pressure, and this pressure is the diastolic blood pressure.

If your blood pressure is 125 over 70, the systolic pressure is 125 and the diastolic pressure is the 70. 125 over 70 by the way, is good.

What is not good is when this blood pressure goes up. High blood pressure is brought about by three factors and they are as follows:

a) Blood viscosity. Viscosity is the thickness of your blood, and this is determined by the ratio of red blood cells to plasma. The higher the ratio of red blood cells to plasma, the thicker your blood, and the more difficult it will be to pump it through your arteries.

b) Total blood vessel length. Resistance to blood flow in your body is directly proportional to the total length of all your blood vessels. The longer the blood vessels, the more resistance you will have to the blood flowing through them. An overweight person may have high blood pressure brought on mostly by the total length of all the blood vessels in their body.

c) Blood vessel diameter (measured from inside wall to inside wall). Resistance to blood flow is inversely proportional to the diameter of the blood vessel, therefore, the smaller the diameter of the blood vessel, the greater the resistance it will offer to the flow of blood. As an example of this relationship, if the diameter of a blood vessel decreases by one half, its resistance to blood flow will increase by at least four times.

People who eat proper nutrition and who exercise regularly are not prone to have high blood pressure, and those who do have high blood pressure will very likely be able to reduce it through regular cardiovascular exercise.

Proper nutrition means eating only those foods that do not contribute to cholesterol buildup, and it means maintaining normal body weight through a proper diet.

High blood pressure is also called hypertension and is usually caused by atherosclerosis. Atherosclerosis frequently has no symptoms and is known to lead to coronary heart disease and strokes.

## Atherosclerosis

What is Atherosclerosis? It is a disease of the arteries, and along with cancer, is the leading cause of death in the western world. It can cause angina, heart attacks, strokes, and gangrene.

Atherosclerosis develops when cholesterol, fat, or fat absorbing cells accumulate as plaque under the inner lining of medium and large arteries, and swell into the artery. This plaque buildup restricts the flow of blood within the artery and causes high blood pressure.

If the blood flow becomes too restricted, any tissues downstream that are supplied by the blocked artery will be in serious trouble.

Plaque can restrict or block arteries anywhere in the body, but it is most common in the arteries that supply the heart.

The vessels that supply the heart are known as coronary arteries and when blockage occurs in these it is known as coronary heart disease. It is the partial or complete blockage of the heart's blood supply in these coronary arteries that can cause angina or a heart attack.

## Angina

Angina is a chest pain resulting from insufficient blood supply to the heart. This is caused by plaque partially blocking the coronary arteries. Even with 60% blockage, the coronary arteries can supply the heart with enough nutrients and oxygen while it is at rest.

During physical activity the heart requires more blood, and if a partially blocked artery will not allow more blood to flow, the muscles of the heart will develop a cramp like pain. This pain in the heart is called angina.

Angina can be brought on by physical activity, sudden exertion, emotional stress or sudden excitement, and should quickly disappear when these conditions are no longer present.

If the coronary arteries are almost completely blocked, you will also have chest pains but they will be much more severe. They will also be of longer duration, and will sometimes result in a heart attack.

This can occur when plaque breaks loose and gets lodged further along the coronary artery where the artery narrows. This can completely block the flow of blood to the heart.

In most cases, however, a heart attack is brought on when a blood clot forms on a plaque, causing the plaque to rupture and releasing substances that increase the clotting effect. This clot then builds up on the ruptured plaque and completely blocks the artery.

To reduce the chance of a clot occurring, your doctor may request that you take a clot inhibitor such as aspirin. Be advised that aspirin may cause you to develop ulcers, and within five years may cause serious damage to your kidneys.

There are natural products on the market that will correct plaque and clotting conditions, and are safe to use. One product that I am familiar with, and use regularly, is Cayenne Pepper. Cayenne pepper dissolves plaque anywhere in your bloodstream, and will keep your pipes absolutely clean with regular use.

Friends of mine report that their chest pains have disappeared and their energy levels have improved through the regular use of nothing more than Cayenne pepper.

Cayenne pepper comes in various strengths, in powder or capsule form, and can be purchased at any Health Food Store. I take two capsules of regular 42,000 SHU cayenne pepper per day to prevent any blockages. Some very positive benefits of this natural product are; no chest pains, plenty of energy, no side-effects, and cayenne pepper is very reasonably priced.

Regular use of cayenne pepper will go a long way toward helping you with high blood pressure, angina, and other conditions caused by restricted blood flow in your arteries.

**Cholesterol**

High blood pressure can also be brought on by high cholesterol. Cholesterol is a type of fat that is an essential element of all the cells in your body. It is especially important to the cells of nerves, the spinal cord, and the brain. Cholesterol is found in all animal food products.

Your liver produces most of the cholesterol used by your body, and your blood carries this cholesterol to the various places in your body where it is needed. To assist with this transportation, the cholesterol binds itself to particles called lipoproteins.

There are two types of lipoproteins, low-density lipoprotein (LDL), and high-density lipoprotein (HDL). It is excessive LDL that causes cholesterol damage in the arteries, and therefore has been termed "bad cholesterol".

HDL transports excess LDL back to the liver for disposal, and because of this has been termed "good cholesterol". Cholesterol can be measured by a blood test, and can be controlled by cardiovascular exercise.

**Stress**

Another problem that can be controlled by exercise is stress. Stress is a disease of our modern society and cannot really be measured because it means different things to different people.

Stress has been defined as the way in which an individual relates to his environment. One person may be totally content to wait at a traffic light while it may drive someone else up the wall.

Learning how to relax is the biggest single thing we can do for stress, and exercising is one of the best ways to do this. If things that you may not have much control over get out of hand, or don't go the way you would like them to, take a deep breath and go for a walk, you'll live a lot longer.

Excess body weight is something else that can be controlled through exercise. Being overweight itself may not be a problem, but overweight usually brings with it high blood pressure, high cholesterol, or diabetes. All three of these can be controlled by weight loss, and as mentioned, weight loss can easily be controlled by exercise.

Other benefits to a regular exercise routine are increased muscle strength, increased bone strength, and greater flexibility in your skeletal joints. All of these can be improved by participating in sports, jogging, cycling, or any other cardiovascular activity that you may choose.

**Your Lymphatic System**

Up to this point we have focused on cardiovascular exercise with the emphasis being on supplying the cells of your body with nutrients and oxygen. There is another very important benefit to exercise, and that is the removal of waste products and toxins from your body.

This waste removal process is carried out by your lymphatic system, and in order to understand how this waste removal works we should take a look at what the lymphatic system is.

Your lymphatic system consists of lymphatic fluid, lymphatic vessels, lymph nodes, the spleen, the tonsils, the thymus gland, and thousands of one-way valves in your lymphatic vessels that control the flow of lymphatic fluid. Your lymphatic system relies on your veins and arteries to help it to remove toxins, and here is how all of this works.

Your heart pumps blood plasma through your arteries to all parts of your body. As these arteries become smaller and smaller they become known as capillaries. Most components of this blood plasma move freely through the capillary walls, and when this occurs this blood plasma enters the region between the cells of your body and becomes known as interstitial fluid. This interstitial fluid carries nutrients, oxygen, and other substances to your cells.

Waste products from these cells - dead cell tissue, spent nutrient products, toxins etc. - are released from the cells into the interstitial fluid. They are carried into the lymphatic capillaries through one-way openings, and are then on their way out of your body.

Once this interstitial fluid enters the lymphatic capillary it becomes known as lymphatic fluid. Figure 5 shows this interstitial fluid, the cells, the lymphatic capillaries, the lymphatic fluid, and the one-way openings in the wall of the lymphatic capillaries.

Figure 6 shows the relationship between the arteries, the blood capillaries (tiny arteries), the lymphatic capillaries, the venules (tiny veins), and the veins. The movement of red blood is from the heart to the arteries, to the capillaries, to the venules, to the veins, and back to the heart.

The movement of nutrients and oxygen is from the arteries, to the capillaries, through the capillary walls, through the interstitial fluid, and into the cells. The blood delivers nutrients and oxygen to the cells of your body in this fashion. The portion of the blood that is not absorbed through the capillary walls continues back to the lungs and the intestines where it is replenished and used again. (See Figure 7.)

The movement of waste products from your cells is through the interstitial fluid, through the openings in the wall of the lymphatic capillaries, through the lymphatic capillaries to the lymphatic vessels, through a series of lymph nodes, and through the lymphatic ducts where the waste products and toxins in your body are emptied into your veins. (Shown in Figures 5, 6, and 7.)

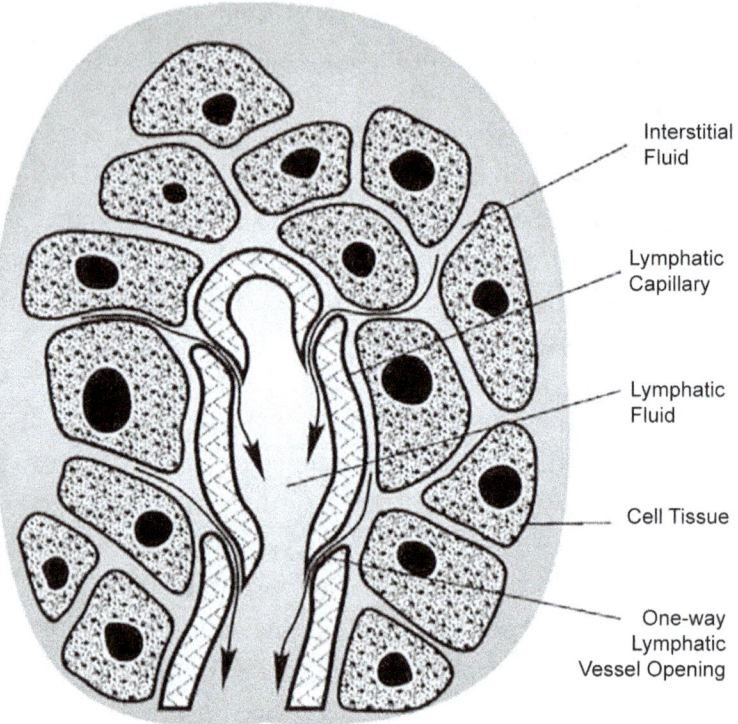

Interstitial Fluid

Lymphatic Capillary

Lymphatic Fluid

Cell Tissue

One-way Lymphatic Vessel Opening

Figure 5. Details of Lymphatic Capillary

These waste products are carried in the lymphatic fluid, which are emptied into your veins through two lymphatic ducts in the vicinity of your collarbones. From the veins, your waste products are carried back to your heart, and are then pumped to your liver and your kidneys where the waste products are filtered from the blood and eliminated from your body.

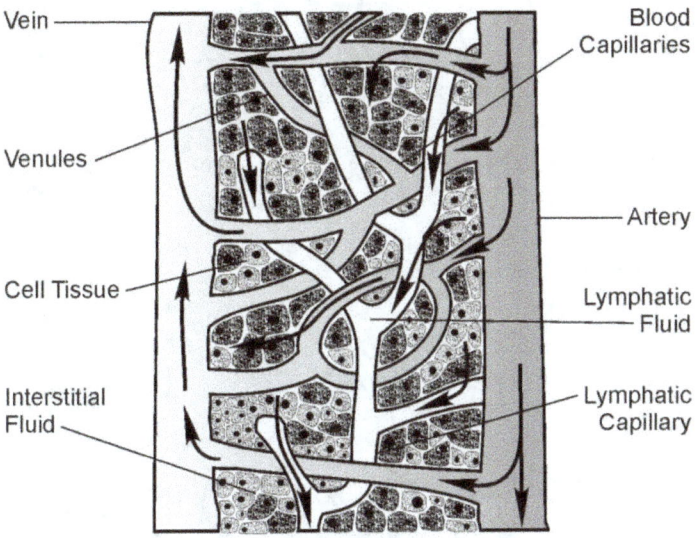

Figure 6. Relationship between arteries, blood capillaries, lymphatic capillaries, venules & veins

The pumping of your heart forces the blood to flow through the arteries, capillaries, venules, and veins, but the movement of lymphatic fluid through the lymphatic capillaries and lymphatic vessels works a little differently.

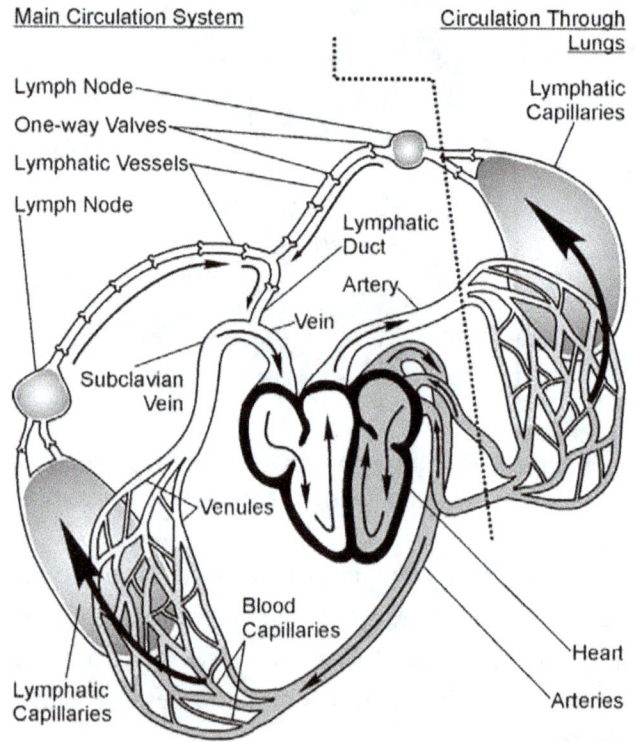

Main Circulation System

Circulation Through Lungs

Lymph Node
One-way Valves
Lymphatic Vessels
Lymph Node
Lymphatic Capillaries
Lymphatic Duct
Artery
Vein
Subclavian Vein
Venules
Blood Capillaries
Lymphatic Capillaries
Heart
Arteries

Arrows show direction of lymph and blood flow

Figure 7.   Relationship between lymphatic system and cardiovascular system

**One-Way Valves**

There are two ways to physically move lymphatic fluid through the lymphatic system, and they are as follows. All along the lymphatic vessels you will find hundreds of one-way lymph nodes and one-way valves. (See Figure 7.) One way simply means that they only allow lymphatic fluid to flow in one direction, and that is away from the cells and toward the veins as described.

These lymphatic vessels are in all parts of your body and are surrounded by muscle tissue. Whenever your muscles contract, they squeeze the lymphatic vessels and force most of the lymphatic fluid out of them. This lymphatic fluid can only move in one direction because of the one-way valves, and so the fluid is forced toward the veins.

When the muscle releases, the lymphatic vessels fill up again until the next muscle contraction. This serves as a pumping action and is one way that lymphatic fluid moves through the lymphatic vessels toward the veins and on to the heart.

The second way is through up and down movement of your body, and that works like this. Most of your lymphatic fluid has to move from your lower extremities and go up to your lymphatic ducts, where your lymphatic fluid is emptied from your lymphatic vessels into your veins.

These lymphatic ducts (the right lymphatic duct and the left lymphatic duct) are situated in the vicinity of your collarbones, and this means that your lymphatic fluid below this level has to move in an upward direction. The lymphatic fluid above this level simply drains downward and is not a problem.

All of your lymph nodes and one-way valves open in a direction that only allows fluid movement toward the lymphatic ducts. By moving up and down in an aerobic type motion this series of one-way valves opens and closes.

When we move in a downward motion the valves open and allow lymphatic fluid to effectively move in an upward direction within your lymphatic vessels. When we move in an upward motion the valves close and fluid movement is stopped. When we again move downward the valves once again open and allow fluid movement in an upward direction.

This up and down movement of your body, in conjunction with your muscles contracting and releasing, works very efficiently at moving lymphatic fluid from your lower extremities upward to your lymphatic ducts, and thereby remove waste products from your body.

**Your Most Effective Exercise**

The most efficient method of removing waste products is by exercising on a mini-trampoline. This up and down motion, combined with the contracting and releasing of large muscle tissue will provide you with cardiovascular exercise, and remove toxins from your body at the same time. The second best form of exercise for your heart and lungs, and for removing waste from your body, is a brisk walk or jogging.

The type of exercise you do is not as important as doing something. Start with some form of aerobic exercise such as walking, swimming, cycling or whatever else you feel comfortable with, and slowly increase your activities from there.

If you do strenuous exercise, try to combine that with some aerobic exercise as well. Strenuous exercise produces more waste products than you eliminate, and these waste products can be removed through aerobic exercise.

**Preventive Medicine**

The human body was designed and built for movement, but our modern lifestyles are not conducive to regular physical activity. Regular exercise is necessary to develop and maintain good levels of health, performance, and appearance; and can improve the overall condition of your body, especially the condition of your heart, lungs, and blood vessels. Physical activity can also provide an outlet for mental fatigue and other job related tensions.

You should look at exercise as being preventive medicine. The human body was designed for physical activity, and if your body is not exercised, it will deteriorate. Your heart will become weaker, your lungs won't function as well, and your muscles will lose their tone. All bodily functions will become less efficient, and your body will become weaker and more vulnerable to many diseases and illnesses.

On the other hand, it is amazing to see what can happen to your body if you do give it regular exercise. It will not only make you look and feel younger, but it will change your whole outlook on life.

Your attitude toward yourself and others will change, you will more easily be able to deal with the stress of life, you will be able to sleep better, and you will also be able to accomplish more during your waking hours.

Kindly allow me to say that just reading about the benefits of exercise won't help you, you have to experience the benefits for yourself. Exercise is just as important as eating, and it should be given the same priority.

You need to make time for your exercise routine whether it is morning, afternoon, or evening, and when you do make the time and exercise regularly, you will feel stronger and you will have more energy.

A brisk walk every day is all the exercise that you really need. It gets your heart beating, and by giving yourself time to think, you get mental exercise as well. Or, if you prefer, you can exercise on a mini-trampoline. A mini-trampoline is excellent for you, because it will give you cardiovascular exercise without the physical stress that is associated with brisk walking or jogging.

Also, as previously mentioned, the up and down motion on a mini-trampoline will greatly assist in removing toxins from your body. Whatever form of exercise you choose, do it on a regular basis and your body will thank you for it.

One other important item to remember is to get enough sleep at night. This gives your body time to rebuild and recover from the damage it has suffered all day. If you do not get enough rest, your immune system will be weak and it will not be able to protect you from the germs, bacteria, and viruses that you come into contact with every day.

Not getting enough sleep is just as serious as not getting proper nutrition, because they both have the same effect on your cells. Not getting enough sleep deprives your body of the time it needs to rebuild your cells, and not getting good nutrition deprives your body of the building materials it needs to replenish those cells.

## Chapter Twelve

# The Workers Within Us

Our body is a complex machine. It was designed so that all the individual parts could work in conjunction with all the other parts to enable us to perform certain functions.

It can be compared to the physical makeup of a modern computer system. Our brain can be compared to the central processing unit (CPU). Our nerve fibers can be compared to the wires or the circuit board runs inside a computer, and our eyes, ears, and hands etc, can be compared to the peripheral equipment that a computer generally controls, such as printers, monitors, etc.

The big difference, of course, is that we are living breathing human beings, and a computer is, after all, only a machine. We are also far more complex than a computer, and our system of operation is much more refined.

To process information, all that a computer is able to work with is a series of zeros and ones, known as a binary code. We have the ability to process much more information, and to obtain that information from many more sources.

To help us process all the information that we accumulate we rely on certain workers within our body that are able to perform certain functions. These functions are accomplished at a cellular level and include the operation of our five senses, keeping the blood flowing in our veins, supplying our cells with oxygen and nutrients, and many other operations too numerous to mention.

The workers we are referring to are enzymes and friendly bacteria, and these two are responsible for most of the work that takes place within our body. We also need certain minerals and vitamins, and the enzymes that we have in our body serve as a catalyst that allow the minerals and vitamins to do their job.

**Enzymes, minerals, and vitamins** are the topic of this chapter and I would like to say a few words about each of these.

**Enzymes**

What are enzymes? Enzymes are organic protein molecules that break down food particles such as proteins, carbohydrates, and fat, and convert them into smaller absorbable nutrients for the building of cells, tissues, and organs.

There are two types of enzymes, digestive enzymes, and metabolic enzymes. Digestive enzymes can be further divided into either plant enzymes or pancreatic enzymes.

Plant enzymes are derived from plants and are very beneficial in that they begin to digest your food in your gastrointestinal tract before it reaches your small intestine. Plant enzymes function in both an acidic and alkaline environment, which makes them more useful under a wider range of conditions. They are not destroyed by acids in your stomach.

Pancreatic enzymes are animal based, and only function in the small intestine.

Metabolic enzymes work as a catalyst. They are the driving force behind the thousands of chemical actions that take place in our body. If it were not for metabolic enzymes, these chemical actions would not take place.

Each enzyme has one specific function that no other enzyme can perform. Because of this, our body requires the full range of enzymes so that all functions within our body can be fulfilled.

Enzymes concentrate iron in the blood, help the blood to coagulate, help to eliminate carbon dioxide from the lungs, assist in the removal of waste material from the body, and are also very active in the rebuilding of new muscle tissue, nerve cells, skin, bone, and glandular tissue.

Enzymes perform most of the functions in our body, and that is why they are referred to as "the workers". We simply cannot survive without them.

One of the most common health problems in North America today is poor digestion. This is brought on by a lack of digestive enzymes being present in the food that we eat, and by our body not producing enough digestive enzymes on its own.

Low levels of enzymes can lead to a toxic colon, and can cause a buildup of toxic by-products that circulate in our bloodstream and affect every cell in our body.

As we age, our body slowly loses its ability to produce enzymes, and for this reason, it is highly recommended that elderly persons supplement their diet with digestive enzymes.

A lot of enzymes are destroyed because of cooking, exposure to light and air, alcohol, caffeine, smoking, pharmaceutical drugs, parasites, ultraviolet radiation, pesticides, pollutants, chlorine and fluoridated water. Of these, chlorine and smoking are the most deadly, because these two can kill every known enzyme in our body. Because of this, all age groups should supplement their diet with plant based enzymes.

## Sources of Enzymes

We can obtain enzymes from three sources. Our body can manufacture its own enzymes, we can obtain enzymes through the food that we eat, or we can obtain enzymes through supplements.

When looking at food as an enzyme source we can look to either herbs, fresh vegetables, or to various fruits. Herbal enzymes are in their natural, unprocessed state, and easily complement the digestive juices that are already active in our body.

Some chlorophyll-rich herbs such as alfalfa, barley grass, chlorella, spirulina, kelp, peppermint and sea vegetables are also a very good source of enzymes.

Most vegetables also provide us with enzymes, but we have to be careful because enzymes are extremely sensitive to heat. Even low to moderate heat, 105 degrees F and above, will destroy most of the enzymes in our food, so to obtain enzymes from these sources we really should eat our food raw. When looking at vegetables, sprouts are the richest sources of enzymes.

E.R. (Ron) Harder

Enzymes can also be found in many fruits. Avocados, papayas, pineapples, bananas, and mangos are all high in enzymes. Unripe papaya and pineapple are the richest sources.

There is one thing you might want to know about enzymes and it is this. You can never get enough enzymes. The more enzymes you consume, the healthier you will be. You cannot overdose on enzymes.

Enzymes are workers, and the more workers you have in your body, the better your digestion and your metabolic functions will be. Taking full spectrum enzymes will guarantee that you are getting the full range of the enzymes that you need.

Be sure to use enzyme supplements that are derived from plants, and that they contain all the eight major enzymes such as protease, amylase, lipase, cellulase, maltase, lactase, phytase, and sucrase.

**Enzyme Summary**

Here is a brief summary of what the eight enzymes do.

PROTEASE - One of the two most important digestive enzymes, and it is responsible for digesting the proteins in your food. This enzyme is very active in helping to defeat cancer.

AMYLASE - The other very important digestive enzyme, and it is responsible for digesting carbohydrates.

LIPASE - Responsible for digesting fats in food, as well as in the arteries.

CELLULASE - Breaks down plant fibers. It also binds to heavy metals and toxins and carries them out of your body. This is a powerful antioxidant.

MALTASE - Changes the complex sugars found in malt products and grains into glucose.

LACTASE - Responsible for digesting milk sugar.

PHYTASE - Assists in digestion and helps to produce vital nutrients from the B-Complex vitamins.

SUCRASE - Responsible for digesting the sugars in our food.

**Minerals**

Minerals are naturally occurring elements found in the earth. The rocks and stones that make up our planet are made from mineral salts that gradually break down into tiny particles because of erosion. This erosion process can take a very long time, but the end result is the formation of dust particles that make up our soil.

This soil, assuming it is healthy, is saturated with microbes that make use of these mineral salts and pass them on to the plants. We then obtain these minerals by consuming those plants.

Every cell in our body depends on minerals for proper bodily functions. They are needed for the makeup of body fluids, for the proper composition of blood and bone material, for healthy nerve fibers, and to control the quality of the muscle tissue.

Minerals function as coenzymes, which assist the body in the production of energy, for growth, and in healing. All enzyme activity involves minerals, which are essential for the proper function of vitamins and nutrients.

The level of different minerals in our body, and in particular the ratio of mineral levels one to another, is what determines the chemical balance. Proper chemical balance is essential to maintaining good health.

**Vitamins**

Vitamins are essential in small quantities for the normal metabolic functioning of your body. Most vitamins cannot be produced by your body and must be obtained from dietary sources, or from supplements. They are classified according to whether they are fat or water-soluble, or by their chemical structures, and are normally designated by letters.

Vitamins are considered micronutrients because your body uses them in much smaller amounts than it uses carbohydrates, proteins, and fats. Vitamins work in conjunction with enzymes to ensure that all the activities that occur within your body are being carried out as required.

## In Summary

Enzymes, minerals, and vitamins are absolutely essential for your health. There is nothing in your body that can take place without enzymes, there can be no growth without minerals, and there can be no chemical reactions without vitamins. These three are responsible for life itself, and you should ensure that all three of these are kept in proper balance in your body.

When attempting to obtain enzymes, minerals, and vitamins from food sources, do your very best to ensure that these sources are organic. As we saw previously, nutrients in commercially grown food are virtually nonexistent.

## Chapter Thirteen

## Improving Your Health

There are a number of things we can do to improve our overall health, and I would like to mention some of them here.

**Clean Your Colon**

To improve your health, you absolutely need to do one very important thing, and that is to clean your colon. This can easily be accomplished by using a product designed for that purpose. Cleansing is absolutely essential if you want to maintain your health, or regain your health.

Eighty years or so ago when our foods still had nutrients and enzymes in them, keeping our colon clean was not a problem because we digested a lot more of the food that we consumed. Today, because of all the chemicals in our food, and the lack of nutrients and enzymes, we are not able to digest most of what we eat, and it accumulates in the colon.

Bowel management is not something that is generally discussed in our society, and in fact is not mentioned at all until a problem develops. We seem to think that the colon will somehow take care of itself, but it is no longer able to do that.

You may be wondering if everybody needs to cleanse, and the simple answer is "YES". Everybody who eats processed foods, frozen foods, canned foods, convenience foods, red meat products etc., will most likely have a fair amount of toxic build-up in their colon, and all of these toxins need to be removed to prevent disease.

These foods are low in fiber, nutrients, and enzymes, and will cause the colon contents to become entrapped in mucus.

Some prominent people in the field of dietary health inform me that out of the thousands of patients they have attended to over the years, not one person, except for someone who is on a colon cleanse, has what they would call a healthy colon.

In order for your colon to be healthy you have to be able to remove the toxins from your body, and this brings us to the most important and probably the least understood function that takes place within us.

**Eliminating Toxins**

The major elimination channels of the body are the colon, the skin, the lymphatic system, and the respiratory system. When the elimination systems of the body are functioning effectively, blood, lymph, and tissue fluids remain relatively clean, which is a prerequisite for good health.

When one or more of these eliminative channels are not functioning properly, the others are forced to compensate and carry the extra load. If they are unable to handle the overload, toxins and waste products find their way back into the bloodstream, recirculate throughout the body and settle in the weakest organs and tissues. This toxicity in the body lays the groundwork for disease.

If we do not eliminate our waste products, we cannot keep our blood clean, and as we have just seen, these toxic compounds will then re-circulate throughout our entire body. As a result of this, our elimination channels will not receive proper nutrition and will not be able to function effectively.

This, in turn, causes more waste products to accumulate, which degrades the elimination systems even more. As you can see, toxic buildup can be an endless degenerative cycle.

## Bowel Elimination

Proper bowel elimination is very important because it has a direct effect on how well the entire body functions. Proper elimination should occur within one hour after a normal meal, and this is brought on in the following manner.

In a healthy person, it takes approximately sixteen to twenty hours to complete the digestive process and move the waste products along the digestive tract and into the bowel. When we eat a normal meal, waste products are moved further along the colon to make room for more material coming from the small intestine.

When we eat a full meal, these newer waste products coming down the intestinal tract will build up pressure in the bowel, and when this pressure reaches a certain level, a bowel movement is triggered. Someone with a healthy colon should experience an elimination process within twenty minutes of eating a meal, and this elimination process should take no more than a few minutes.

The waste of what we eat today should be removed by an elimination process tomorrow, and if this does not occur, these waste products will accumulate in your colon, your colon will become toxic, and this is an invitation for parasites to grow.

There are a variety of parasites in all natural food and water, and the parasite incubation period is approximately thirty-six hours, therefore, you can expect parasites to develop in your colon if you do not have a regular elimination cycle. (As a matter of interest, the average digestion/elimination process for North Americans is approximately seventy-two hours.)

**Improve Your Digestion**

The colon is an organ just like any other in your body and it thrives on quality nutrition. You can improve digestion and help your colon perform its functions by doing the following:

a) Practice good eating habits, such as chewing your food well and eating slowly.

b) Relax after eating to promote digestion.

c) Eat smaller, more frequent meals to promote better digestion.

d) Drink water or beverages with your meal.

e) Eat only top quality food that your body can use.

f) Help your digestive system by taking digestive enzyme supplements derived from plants.

g) Help your elimination system by using a special colon food/cleanser as described in a later chapter.

h) Eat as much raw food and whole food as possible.

For those who are not familiar with raw food and whole food, there is now a lot of information available on the Internet about raw food, whole food, their benefits, and how to prepare it.

Consuming raw/organic/whole food ensures that you will get the nutrients and enzymes that your body requires, and you will get food that is as close to toxin free as possible.

Of all the organs, the colon has the most effect on all parts of your body. It is the one organ with the greatest accumulation of toxins, and therefore should be the one organ that receives the greatest amount of care.

Colon cancer and other digestive tract diseases are rampant in North America and might easily be prevented by proper food selection, proper digestive habits, and proper bowel management.

Think of your body as a system with many different parts. In order to function properly, each of these parts requires a certain quantity and quality of fuel. The fuel that you give your body comes from the food that you eat, and your food should contain the essential nutrients that will allow you to maintain your good health.

It is these nutrients that allow you to sustain life by providing you with the basic materials that your body needs. All nutrients have different specific functions and are involved in bodily processes ranging from fighting infection to tissue repair. If you do not provide your body with proper nutrition, you will impair your body's metabolic functions and cause yourself a great deal of harm.

**What Not To Eat**

To be able to choose the proper foods, and to be able to understand why those foods are so important, you need to have a clear understanding as to the ingredients of a healthy diet.

When planning a healthy diet, knowing WHAT NOT TO EAT is just as important as knowing WHAT TO EAT, and to help you with that I have included a short list of foods that you should avoid.

a)  Avoid all sugar products. Your body produces all the sugar it needs, and any refined sugar you give it is really a poison to your system because of all the chemicals that are added to it.

Excessive sugar intake, along with being overweight, is the major causes of diabetes. Also, as you saw in a previous chapter, sugar is pure food for any bacterial diseases you may have in your intestinal tract.

b) Avoid artificial sweeteners. Artificial sweeteners such as aspartame (NutraSweet, Equal, and Spoonful) are very popular. They are about twenty times sweeter than sugar and can be found in the following products: Instant breakfasts, breath mints, cereals, sugar-free chewing gum, cocoa mixes, coffee beverages, frozen desserts, gelatin desserts, juice beverages, laxatives, milk drinks, multivitamins, shake mixes, soft drinks, tabletop sweeteners, tea beverages, instant tea and coffee, topping mixes, wine coolers, and yogurt.

Aspartame consists of three major components; the amino acids phenylalanine, aspartic acid, and methanol, also known as methyl alcohol. The amino acids in aspartame are suspected of causing brain damage under certain conditions, and the methanol is known to be poisonous even when consumed in very small quantities. Toxic levels of methanol cause blindness, brain swelling, and inflammation of the pancreas and heart.

The Food and Drug Administration (FDA) states that exposure to methanol through aspartame is not of sufficient quantity to cause concern, but, a large number of people have reported ill effects from aspartame consumption including headaches, mood swings, vision problems, nausea, diarrhea, sleep disorders, memory loss, and convulsions. Aspartame is harmful for adults, and is especially deadly for children.

c) Avoid all white flour products, white rice, crackers, cold cereals, and instant oatmeal. White flour products produce mucus in the intestines, which will allow parasites to grow. This mucus also coats your intestinal wall, and restricts the ability of your intestines to absorb nutrients.

To give you an idea of what white flour will do, mix a bit of it with water and stir it until it thickens. The kids back in school used this as a paste, and I know that my ancestors mixed this stuff up and used it as a glue with which to hang wallpaper. Imagine what this does to your intestines.

d) Avoid commercially canned food. Canned food has chemicals added to it to prevent the food from spoiling while it sits on the shelf. If this food will not break down and decay on the shelf, how can it break down and be digested in your small intestine.

e) Avoid all soft cheeses, colored cheeses, all pasteurized products including milk, margarine, commercial ice cream, saturated fats, shortenings, and processed oils.

f) Avoid alcoholic drinks, coffee, cocoa, and regular tea.

g) Avoid all forms of pork, red meat, beef, hot dogs, processed meats, and organ meats. Our body was not designed to digest meat products, and because of that, the meat that you consume will sit in your digestive tract and ferment. If it is not removed by cleansing, it will turn toxic and spread all kinds of bacteria and toxins throughout your entire body.

h) Use only small amounts of black or white pepper, or salt. Excessive sodium input has been known to cause high blood pressure, and contribute to congestive heart failure.

I estimate that only about 10% of all the products sold in an average grocery store are good for you, and most of this can be found in the fruit and vegetable department. The other 90% can and does hurt you.

Our diet in North America consists largely of processed foods, canned foods, and convenience foods, which have been prepared with all kinds of chemicals.

We consume all these processed foods and expect our digestive system to be able to cope with it year after year. We load up on dairy foods that have been pasteurized and homogenized, and we don't realize that these processes destroy any nutrients that ever were in these foods.

**What To Eat**

Before you get too depressed, let me mention the foods that our body CAN use. These include, but are not limited to, the following.

a) Eat only whole/organic food, or food that is as close to organic as possible.

b) Try to eat your vegetables raw if possible.

c) Eat plenty of fresh fruit.

d) Eat plenty of fresh raw nuts.

e) Drink herbal teas, fresh vegetable and fruit juices, or alkaline water.

f) Eat goat cheese, nonfat cottage cheese, unsweetened yogurt, goat's milk, buttermilk, rice milk, and most soy products.

g) Eat only whole grain products when eating cereals, breads, oats, brown rice, or wild rice.

h) Eat only freshwater white fish, broiled or baked salmon, water-packed tuna, and fish with fins and scales.

i) Eat only boiled or poached eggs.

j)  Use only cold-pressed oils, either corn, safflower, sesame, olive, flaxseed, soybean, or sunflower oils. Use butter instead of margarine.

k)  Use garlic, onions, cayenne pepper, all herbs, apple cider vinegar, tamari, seaweed, or dulse.

l)  Eat homemade soups that are salt and fat free.

m)  And very important! Please refer to Chapter Nine and try to follow the food charts, keeping in mind the 80/20 rule for alkaline/acidic foods.

It is important that we are aware of everything that is going into our body. Consume fresh fruits, and either raw vegetables, or vegetables that have been lightly steamed. Poultry and fish, whole grains and nuts, are all nutritious foods. Try to eat your food in its raw form so that you can benefit from the live enzymes that are in it.

We are the most overfed, and yet undernourished society in the world. We don't seem to fully understand that quality natural foods are the "Life Force" in our body. The foods we eat without this "Life Force" do nothing but clog up our digestive system.

Good food burns thoroughly and low grade food leaves a residue, and this residue adds work to the digestive and elimination systems. Because it leaves a residue, low grade food adds considerably to the degeneration of your body. It has been said that "Death Begins In The Colon", and it is becoming more evident that this is true.

## Food Preparation

There is one very important aspect to food that we have not yet covered and that is the process of preparation. We know that heating our food above a very low temperature (105 degrees F) destroys the enzymes that are in them, but what most of us do not know is that when foods, particularly meat products, are heated to the point of browning or charring, the organic compounds in them undergo a change in structure that produces carcinogens.

Barbecuing meat, for example, seems to be the biggest health threat because when amino acids and chemicals that are found in meat are subjected to high temperatures, dangerous carcinogens are formed. Meat is high in protein, especially red meat, and many of the chemicals used to develop cancer in laboratory animals have been obtained from burned protein. Burned protein is inside all that black stuff that hangs from that barbecued steak or hamburger that people consume.

Anything that is overheated or burned can produce carcinogenic substances, and the dangers of this should not be taken lightly. By way of comparison, eating only half a gram of burned material is equivalent to smoking two packs of cigarettes a day.

Eating raw produce is by far the most beneficial for your body, and your chances of obtaining cancer will be greatly reduced if you do not consume overcooked or barbecued foods.

While we are on the subject of cooking, I would like to suggest that you not use aluminum cookware to prepare your meals. Use only stainless steel, glassware, or iron pots and pans.

Aluminum leaches from the cookware into your food, and this is absorbed into your bloodstream. It then accumulates in your brain and slows down circulation, which is a major cause of Alzheimer's. Aluminum in your body also attacks your nervous system.

In this chapter we have discussed some very simple steps that we need to follow to improve our health, and the biggest of these steps is to clean our body internally and provide it with proper nutrition. In the next chapter we will talk specifically about the steps that we must take to defeat any disease that we may have.

## Chapter Fourteen

# Defeating Cancer

We have covered a lot of material in this book, and all of it has been included to provide us with the information we need so that we can better understand the reasons for the process that we will discuss in this chapter.

The first part of this book covered the subject of WHY we develop disease, and it talked in detail about the importance of compatibility when it comes to the things that we consume.

In the next section we looked at HOW disease develops in our body, mostly because of the action of the Autonomic Nervous System.

We now come to the more important chapter of this book, and in this chapter we will discuss the steps that you need to follow so that you can achieve any level of health that you desire, and defeat any disease that you may have, including cancer.

It is not that difficult to defeat cancer. The difficult part is believing that you CAN defeat it, and then making the commitment to DO it. One other thing. We can have all the information we need to help us to defeat disease, but if we do not take action, there is no way that this information can help us. Knowing how is one thing, taking action is another.

Of all the diseases that we come into contact with, it seems that cancer is the most common. The most common forms of treatment for cancer have been chemo, radiation or surgery, but it seems that these forms of treatment do not defeat the disease, they only alleviate the symptom.

**Defeating Cancer**

There are four basic steps that you will need to follow in order for you to either prevent cancer from happening within you, or defeating any cancer that you may have. These four steps are absolutely essential to good health, and I would like to say a few words about each of them here. The four steps are as follows.

1. **Clean Your Body.**

2. **Feed Your Body.**

3. **Alkalize Your Body.**

## 4. Exercise Your Body.

There are two parts to cleaning your body. The first part has to do with removing toxins from your colon, and the second part involves removing toxins from your cells. We have covered a lot of this in the previous chapters of this book, but I would like to expand on some of the details of cleansing.

## 1. Clean Your Body

**Remove toxins from your colon.**

In a previous chapter we looked at how the colon works and why it plays such an important role in our health. It is extremely important to remove all the toxins that have accumulated in our colon so that our Autonomic Nervous System can provide stimulating nerve impulses to all the organs, glands and tissues in our body.

In other words... by removing the toxins that have accumulated in our colon, we are removing the **CAUSE** of any disease that we may have. Removing the toxins means using special natural health products that have been formulated to remove toxic waste products from the intestinal tract. This is absolutely essential if you want to regain your health. **Stop causing the disease**, and that by itself will go a long way toward helping you heal.

In an earlier chapter we talked about how toxins accumulate in our colon, and we now know how important it is for these toxins to be removed. When selecting a product, try to ensure that it is a blend of herbs designed to be a colon cleanse, along with being a colon food. This will allow us to gently remove the compacted fecal matter from our colon, along with providing nutrition for our intestines.

Disease cannot develop or grow on healthy tissue, so as our intestines heal they will become less and less susceptible to disease. Within a week or two after taking a good colon cleanse product, you will notice that your digestion has improved, and that your elimination process has become much easier, and more regular.

In most cases, the compacted waste material has been accumulating on your colon wall for many years, and it is not at all unreasonable that it should take some time before it is all removed. For someone who has a large build-up of compacted material in their colon, it could take up to one year or more for the bulk of this material to be removed by this herbal cleansing process.

How can you tell if your intestines are being cleansed? Most people who actively cleanse report seeing the results in the waste material that they eliminate almost immediately. The material that has been in your intestines for a long time will be dark in color and will be quite firm. As you cleanse, this waste material will become lighter in colour and be less firm.

Also, compacted fecal matter that has been in your intestines for a long time has gone putrid and will have a very unpleasant odor attached to it. Once your colon has been cleansed, this unpleasant odor will largely disappear.

There is one other item I would like to mention about this method of cleansing. We discussed diverticula pockets in an earlier chapter, and we saw how they can develop into cancer. When we use a good quality product to clean our colon, we are removing a small amount of waste material at a time from our colon wall.

As we get down to removing most of it, we will come into contact with the sections of our colon wall that may have diverticula pockets in them. Continue to cleanse until all the waste material has been removed, including the waste material that has accumulated in the diverticula pockets. Removing these pockets can prevent disease conditions such as colon cancer from developing.

If you start by using too much colon cleansing product per day, you may find that you will experience diarrhea or frequent elimination. Reduce the amount until a stable elimination pattern has developed. Then increase the amount until you find the level that is right for you.

Everybody's body functions a little differently, and so the amount that may be right for you will be too much for someone else, and vice versa.

**Crohn's Disease**

Besides colon cancer, there are other very serious disease conditions that can easily develop because of a toxic colon, and one of them is something called Crohn's Disease. Crohn's Disease is a serious inflammation that most often occurs in your large intestine, it is very painful, and can become life threatening because of all the toxins that it generates.

If this toxic condition is not taken care of by cleaning your colon, inflammation can develop to the point where your doctor may well insist that you have your colon removed, in an effort to save your life. You now do not have a colon to store your compacted fecal matter in preparation for elimination, and what you are now forced to do is to wear something called a colostomy bag. This is a bag that you wear outside your body to capture your compacted fecal matter as it is eliminated. It is not something that anyone would look forward to.

Since most disease conditions within us originate as a result of a toxic colon, absolutely everybody in our society should be involved in some form of colon cleanse. I would recommend that you use a good herbal colon cleanse product so that your colon can be thoroughly cleansed, and can remain disease free.

Your doctor may suggest that you should be doing something called colonics to clean your colon, but I would urge you not to follow that advice, except in an emergency situation. Colonics involves putting a tube inside your rectum and flushing the compacted fecal matter out of your colon using water pressure. This is a mechanical intrusion into your colon and could cause physical damage to your colon wall. It is much safer and more effective to use a herbal colon cleanse product to remove compacted fecal matter.

A good herbal cleansing product will gradually remove the compacted fecal matter from your colon wall a small layer at a time until all the compacted fecal matter has been removed. Above that, a good product will also provide nutrition to your intestinal walls to ensure that your intestinal walls can once again be healthy, and be able to pass on nutrients to your blood vessels.

**Extended Colon**

There is another very important item I would like to mention, and it is this. There are a number of people walking around who have what is commonly called a pot-belly (extended mid-section). At first glance it would seem that these persons, male and female, are simply fat, or overweight. But if you look closer, you will notice that other parts of their body are normal in size, except for their midsection, which can be quite large. What you are really seeing is an expanded colon. Allow me to explain.

Our colon is normally about two and a half inches in diameter. When we consume a lot of red meat and other compounds that we cannot digest, this undigested material will cling to our colon wall, and it will not be removed via a normal bowel movement. As we accumulate more of this material on our colon wall, our colon will expand because of the added material, and it will become ballooned or expanded.

As time goes by, our colon keeps expanding, and it can expand from two inches to eight inches in diameter in a short period of time. The expansion of our colon wall has to go somewhere, and it will be noticed first as an extended stomach.

It may appear that we have gotten fat, but what has really happened is that we now have an extended colon. This may cause us a great deal of pain and discomfort, and can easily lead to the formation of diverticula pockets, irritable bowel syndrome, colon cancer, and other nasty conditions.

If the colon has expanded and a lot of fecal matter is clinging to the walls, this fecal matter will start to ferment and will become diseased. The only material that is being removed from the colon during a bowel movement will be a small channel in the center of the colon. The rest of this material will remain attached to the colon wall, until such time as we take action to remove it with a colon cleanse product.

A good colon cleanse will remove a small portion of this compacted matter at a time, layer by layer, until all of this matter has been removed. Once your colon is clean, your autonomic nervous system can once again provide stimulating nerve impulses to all the organs and glands in your body, and you can regain your health. This is one reason why cleansing your colon is so very important.

If you have an extended colon, use an increased amount of whatever cleansing product you are using to remove the compacted fecal matter from your colon wall. Get your colon back down to a normal size, allow it to perform its proper function, lose weight, get active, and get healthy.

**Fasting**

It has been said that fasting is the ultimate diet, and there is a lot of truth to that, although that is not its primary purpose.

Here is how this works. Your body uses a lot of energy to digest the food that you consume. If your food consumption is large, you may not have a lot of energy left for other body functions, such as removing toxins.

The primary purpose of fasting is to give your body an opportunity to devote most of its energy toward removing toxins from your body instead of digesting food. Try going on a fast for one day out of every seven, and you will be surprised at how your health will improve. Give your body a chance to clean house naturally by fasting.

There are several methods of fasting, but I believe that the most effective method is to drink only water during the duration of the fast, and do not consume any food products. Combine this with using the colon cleanse product during the other six days of the week, and the combination of these two cleansing methods will give your health a dramatic boost.

A lot of information is available on fasting, and you may want to do a search on the web so that you can obtain up to date information on this subject.

**Eliminating Toxins From Your Cells**

This is the second part of cleaning our body, and for this we use special "tools" that have been formulated to help us to bring our body back into something called "homeostasis". (Balance and Harmony.) These tools are Enzymes, and Probiotics.

Please be aware that the enzymes and the probiotics serve a dual purpose. They clean our body by eliminating toxins from our cells, and they feed our body by providing the protein molecules necessary to help us with our digestion, and all of our metabolic functions. In this way they dramatically empower the healing of our body.

Please note: We can eliminate the toxins from our body, and we can use the special tools to help us to get healthy, but if we keep putting toxic substances back into our body, we may GET healthy, but we will not STAY healthy.

**The Workers**

An important part of helping your body to heal has to do with making sure you have sufficient amounts of enzymes and probiotics in your body to perform certain vital functions. These are discussed in the following paragraphs.

**Enzymes**

There are two types of enzymes, digestive enzymes and metabolic enzymes. We discussed enzymes in Chapter Twelve, and so we won't spend too much time on them here, except to say that we have only mentioned the eight major ones. There are many more that your body produces, and they all perform specific functions. Enzymes provide the catalyst that allow all metabolic functions within your body to take place. Enzymes are a very important product in your fight against disease, and should be a product that you use a lot of.

Here are a few more reasons to use enzymes. Enzymes in your body break down your amino acids small enough so that they can be completely digested, because undigested amino acids turn into toxins in your bowel.

You need enzymes so that you can get protein, you need protein to make your minerals work, and you need minerals to make sure your vitamins function. Without enzymes, none of these vital functions would occur.

**Probiotics**

Probiotics are a blend of live friendly bacteria that work in conjunction with the enzymes in your body to help you defeat disease. Probiotics attack unfriendly organisms, including E-coli, and help to build up beneficial bacteria in your colon.

Probiotics are also very active in eating up toxic waste materials that accumulate not only in your colon, but in any other regions of your body where toxins may be present. This helps to clean up your digestive tract, and also helps to control dangerous bacteria, yeast, and viruses that can grow in your intestines.

Probiotics will dramatically strengthen your immune system to help your body defeat disease. They are just as important as the enzymes, and also help to control candida buildup in your body.

**Your Army**

You could think of the enzymes and the probiotics as being the army in your body that helps you to fight disease. The enzymes play a key role in getting your metabolism working, and the probiotics are your immune system.

Think of it this way. You have all this disease and toxic material in your body that you are trying to get rid of, and your immune system has been overwhelmed. Things look pretty bleak… and then along comes your army in the form of enzymes and probiotics to help you fight your war.

You may have developed some disease condition that has slowly been taking control over your body, but now you have your army with you to give you a hand. The stronger your army, the quicker you will be able to defeat the enemy that you have within you.

If you have ten million toxic bacteria in your body that have taken control, and you are trying to defeat them with what may be left of your immune system, you will lose. It is that simple. You have to build up your army to help you win the war.

The more enzymes and probiotics you consume, the quicker you will be able to defeat whatever disease condition you may have. Smaller amounts may not work as well for you. Your life might be at stake, so build up your army, turn them loose in your body, let them go to work for you, and help them get the job done. The idea is to defeat your disease, before it defeats you.

When purchasing enzymes, ensure that they contain all the eight major enzymes in one capsule. These will provide the most benefit to you. A very important part of this program is to remove the toxins from your cells. The enzymes and probiotics will help you do that.

## 2. Feed Your Body

Feeding your body is all about providing your body with the nutrition that it needs to build new healthy cell tissue. Providing your body with nutritional food is a two-part process. Part one has to do with changing your diet, and part two has to do with using special natural health supplements that have been formulated to help you rebuild your cells as quickly as possible.

You have to ensure that whatever you put into your body is of the highest quality, and for that reason the only type of food you should be eating is organic, and raw organic food if possible.

There is one other item I would like to mention about organic food. I mentioned earlier about not putting anything into your body that is not compatible with your electrical makeup. Raw/organic food is as close as you are going to get when you look for food that is compatible with your molecular matrix.

Raw/organic food by itself may not provide you with sufficient quality nutrition to help you to rebuild your cell structure in a short period of time, and therefore, I would like to recommend that you consume nutritional supplements that have been formulated to supply the nutrients that your body requires for optimum health.

You may wish to refer to Chapter Thirteen, under the section "What To Eat" for a list of food products that are beneficial for you. You might also want to visit your local Health Food Store for information on nutritional foods for you.

## 3. Alkalize Your Body

As we saw in Chapter Nine, alkalizing our body is very important if we want to achieve a high level of health. I cannot over-emphasize the importance of this one item. It is now generally accepted that disease cannot flourish in an alkaline environment, it can only flourish within us if our body is in an acidic condition.

In Chapter Nine we spoke about keeping the PH level of your body at around 7.0, and why this is so critical to your health. There are a few basic things you can do to accomplish that, and they are as follows:

Do not drink any form of soda pop. These drinks are very acidic with a PH of 3.0 to 4.0, and will keep the PH level of your body at 5.0 or lower. Drink only fruit juices or alkaline water, or other liquids that you know are not acidic.

There are a number of companies that market water units that will provide alkaline water with a PH value of up to 9.5 and beyond. You might want to search the web for these listings.

Please be aware of the PH value of the foods that you consume, and try to follow the 80 - 20 rule as closely as possible. Kindly refer to Chapter Nine of this book for details.

## 4. Exercise Your Body

This is a very important step to help you heal and was discussed in Chapter Eleven, and so we won't spend a lot of time on it here. Exercise has many benefits for your health and should be done on a daily basis. Start with something small and easy and build up from there. Your body will thank you for it.

### Help Your Body Heal

The only way that you are going to get rid of any disease is to give your body the "tools" that it needs to do the job. These tools consist of the Colon Cleanse, Enzymes, Probiotics, Pure Complete Nutrition, Alkaline products that will keep your PH level neutral, and Exercise.

The colon cleanse will help to clean toxins out of your body. The enzymes will get your metabolism working, help you to clean your cells, and combat disease. The probiotics will help to eat up toxic waste products. The pure complete nutrition will provide your body with the nutrients that it needs to rebuild your cell structure, alkalizing your body will ensure that further disease does not flourish within you, and exercise will ensure that your nutrients are being delivered to your cells, and waste products are being removed from your body.

As you can see, getting healthy and staying healthy is not really all that difficult. All you have to do is give your body the help it needs, keep your body clean internally, provide it with quality nutrition, exercise regularly, and your body will do the rest.

Your body was designed to heal itself, and it will do this job very nicely if only you will give it half a chance. Leave the healing of your body up to your body, and help your body all that you can. Help it by following a proper diet, and by using the special herbal nutritional health products that have been formulated to help you heal. And help it by following the four steps in this chapter.

**It's Up To You**

Please be aware that you can achieve any level of health that you desire. The most important part is to start by removing the toxins from your body. This alone will make a huge difference in how you feel. It will provide you with more energy, it will cause you to lose weight, and it will give you a much more positive outlook on life. Even if you do nothing else, it is absolutely essential that you clean your colon. Use the colon cleanse methods described above to help you achieve this.

The next simple step is to change your diet. Leave all the junk food alone, and focus on consuming quality nutrition that will nourish you, and use the "workers" mentioned above. This will also go a long way toward improving your health.

Please pay attention to the alkaline level of your body. As mentioned above, this plays an important role in your overall level of health.

It has been said that there are no incurable diseases, there are only incurable people. If someone is not willing to give up the things that have caused them to become ill, they will have a very tough time trying to defeat their disease. They must be willing to make the changes in their lifestyle that will give their body the opportunity to heal.

**Cannabis Oil**

There is one other effective method by which you can defeat your cancer, and that is through the use of Cannabis Oil, better known as CBD. CBD used to have a bad stigma in the health field, but because it has proven to be such an effective healing herb most of that stigma is now gone.

CBD has been marketed successfully as a method to relieve pain, depression, stress, and anxiety, and it has now proven itself to be effective at defeating cancer as well. It is processed from the marijuana plant, and is one of over 100 chemical compounds known as cannabinoids found in this plant.

CBD oil is made by extracting CBD from the cannabis plant, then diluting it with a carrier oil like coconut or hemp seed oil to formulate what is called cannabis oil, a popular natural remedy used for many common ailments.

There is also something called Tetrahydrocannabinol (THC), which is the main psychoactive cannabinoid found in cannabis, and causes the sensation of getting "high" that's often associated with marijuana. A good formulator will be able to remove most of the THC, and increase the elements in the oil that contain the healing properties (CBD). Unlike THC, CBD is not psychoactive.

This quality makes CBD an appealing option for those who are looking for relief from pain and other symptoms without the mind-altering effects of marijuana or certain pharmaceutical drugs.

Cannabis oil was declared illegal for many years, but because of public pressure that label has been removed, and it is now a legal substance in many parts of North America. It can now be purchased legally in some parts of the US, and in all provinces in Canada.

What we believe to be healing properties within the cannabis oil are little more than an exceptional ability of the cannabis oil to destroy cancer cells and toxins in your body. By destroying the cancer cells and the toxins, and removing them from your body, the cannabis oil is providing a huge boost to your immune system, thereby giving your immune system the opportunity to help your body heal.

This would explain why cannabis oil is so effective in helping us to defeat cancer. Destroy the toxins that are trying to kill you, remove them from your body, and your body will no longer manufacture cancer cells to capture and contain the toxins within you.

I am totally convinced of the benefits of cannabis oil, and if I am ever diagnosed with cancer, or any other life-threatening disease, that is what I will be using.

Why was cannabis oil illegal? Because it is processed from the marijuana plant; you cannot patent the marijuana plant, and so, the pharmaceutical companies are not able to control the cannabis oil, or profit from it.

Defeating cancer with CBD is only part of the program, and it can be an effective first step. The other part is to change your lifestyle so that the cancer does not return. In other words, Stop Causing The Problem, and the problem will go away.

For those who have an interest in cannabis oil, you might want to Google "Cannabis Oil" on the internet. There is a lot of information available on cannabis oil, including how to use it to defeat cancer, and where you might be able to obtain it in your area.

*\*\**

This is the end of *How to Prevent and Defeat Cancer Naturally*. I sincerely hope that you will use the information in this book so that you can defeat whatever disease condition you may be faced with. You can defeat your cancer, it's just a matter of making up your mind to do it, and then get it done.

We are ultimately all responsible for what we put into our body, and we are also all responsible for our own health. It is up to each of us to become better informed as to our health options, and to take more responsibility for our own well-being.

Thank you for allowing me to share with you the information in this book. It is my sincere desire that you will use the information on these pages to help yourself to defeat whatever disease condition you may be faced with, especially cancer, and get back to living your life.

In closing, I would like to ask you to take very good care of yourself, be your own best friend, be happy, and be well.

# *Obtaining Supplements*

It can be difficult trying to locate top quality Nutritional Supplements. I would like to suggest a few options. One option would be to obtain your supplements from your local Natural Health Food store. Try to make certain that they will supply you with top quality organic herbal supplements that are designed to clean your body, feed your body, and help your body heal.

If you cannot locate top quality cleansing, probiotic, and enzyme products at your local health food store, another option might be to go online and check to see what they might have on Amazon. They may well carry a complete line of organic products. A third option might be to Google Natural Health Supplements, and see what you might find online.

If you are located in Canada or the USA, you could obtain top quality health supplements from a company called Avena Originals. Avena carries a colon cleanse product called Herb Cocktail, and an excellent line of Probiotics and Full Spectrum Enzymes. Avena is the only company I am aware of that carries the

"Electrically Compatible Nutritional Supplements" that we discussed previously.

Avena also carries a full line of other top quality nutritional products. For more information on the Avena line of health products, kindly contact their office, and they will be happy to assist you.

Their head office is located in Red Deer, Alberta, Canada. If you would like information on AVENA and their complete line of nutritional products, kindly visit their web site at www.avenaoriginals.com, or call 1-800-207-2239.

# *About The Author*

The author was born and raised in a farming community on the Canadian prairies. He was accepted into the Royal Canadian Air Force at the age of seventeen and graduated from the Air Force Academy as an Electronics Engineering Technologist specializing in Radar Systems and Wide-Band Communications. After four years in the Air Force he embarked on a twenty-five year civilian career in Electronics Technology, focusing on Data Processing Systems.

In 2005 he entered into a long-term concentrated study of Natural Health, Nutrition, Anatomy and Physiology, with the emphasis being on the "Electrical Compatibility" between the foods that we consume and the matrix of the human body.

Reference material for this study included many Bachelor of Science textbooks dealing with Anatomy, Physiology and Nutrition. Other study material included books and other material written by prominent Nutritional Scientists who specialize in formulating "Electrically Compatible Nutritional Supplements".

Also included in this study were the completion of an Iridology training program in 2007, and the completion of a Nutritional Health program in 2011.

His twenty-five years of Electronics Engineering Technology background, combined with the concentrated study of Natural Health, Nutritional Health, Anatomy, Physiology, and Iridology have provided the credentials necessary to write this book.

Continuing studies are now focused on additional forms of Natural Hygiene and Natural Healing.